JOHN YARRINGTON

BUILDING THE
YOUTH CHOIR
TRAINING &
MOTIVATING
Teenage
SINGERS

AUGSBURG FORTRESS • MINNEAPOLIS

BUILDING THE YOUTH CHOIR
Training and Motivating Teenage Singers

Material in chapter six contains excerpts from unpublished workshop notes and the article "The Development of a Contemporary, Eclectic Theory for the Training and Cultivation of the Junior High School Male Changing Voice" copyright © John Cooksey. Used by permission.

Cover design: Carol Evans-Smith. Illustration: Terry Boles.

Library of Congress Cataloging-in-Publication Data

Yarrington, John, 1941 -
        Building the youth choir   :   training & motivating teenage singers/
John Yarrington.
                p.   cm.
        Includes bibliographical references.
        ISBN 0-8066-2454-X
        1. Choral singing—Juvenile—Instruction and study. 2. Choirs
        (Music)   I. Title.
        MT915.Y33   1990   90-23
        782.5′2214—dc20   CIP
                                                                         MN

Manufactured in the U.S.A.   AF 11-5215

03   02   01   00   3   4   5   6   7   8   9   10

CONTENTS

INTRODUCTION

In 1980, Choristers Guild published a small volume entitled *Sound Recipes for Teenage Voices*, based on this author's experience with junior and senior high young people at McFarlin United Methodist Church in Norman, Oklahoma—a suburban, middle-class college community of 70,000 with three Methodist churches, two middle schools and one high school. These were years of learning, experimenting, reading, gleaning from others, and growing in the experience of working with young people in a church choir setting, and it was valuable to document principles which worked in that situation. The high school choir in Norman, the "Chapel Choir," began a tradition of touring at year's end. Through the experience of touring the choir established a reputation, and frequently its director was invited to teach workshops and conduct youth choir camps and festivals. Everywhere, it seemed, directors were asking the same questions:
1. How do I get started?
2. What techniques work to establish sound?
3. What music is suitable?
4. How much private or class voice work is practical?
5. Changing voices—what do I do?
6. To tour or not to tour?

Looking back on my years in Norman, I realize how fortunate I was. Since it was possible for young people to get to the church after school, private and class voice work flourished and the choir was better because of it. The relationships fostered in those one-on-one situations made a great difference in the group dynamic. A tradition of a large ninth through twelfth grade choir which sang every Sunday at 8:45 a.m. and took annual tours was kept alive for a period of thirteen years. These same youth were equally active in United Methodist Youth Fellowship activities, and the operative word between the music staff and the youth staff was "cooperation." Parental support was strong and the church was justifiably proud of its Chapel Choir. In many ways it was an ideal situation, though drugs, peer pressure, school pressure, cars, jobs, soccer, and the like were certainly not unknown.

From 1979 to 1989 I served at the First United Methodist Church in Dallas, Texas—a downtown setting, not suburban, in a metroplex population of over one million. There young people for the youth choir, the "Variations," came from numerous junior and senior high schools across the area. Gone was the luxury of after-school time. We were limited to one hour on Sunday afternoon (a day of rest?). Previously there had been two choirs, junior and senior high. But, because of numbers *and* scheduling, we combined the groups into one choir, seventh through twelfth. This grouping seems to be a common one in many churches across the country. In Norman, the group dynamic so important to *everything* was made easier by the setting. It was fostered by "personal relationship time" after school—between director and members, and among the members themselves. In Dallas, achieving a group dynamic was almost more important than developing a sound. These seventh through twelfth graders were together as a group *only* for the one hour a week they spent in choir. Even in youth activities they were separated. They were in different schools all week and, though some were together, the majority had little if any personal inter-action except for choir and youth fellowship. I had to learn that what I took for granted in Norman had to be nurtured intentionally in Dallas: "What doth it profit a group to sound good, if they don't care for each other, know each other, and work together *for* each other" (Yarrington 1:1). On one weekend retreat, for instance, time was given for group-building exercises designed to strengthen the group. On tour, a "Group Time" was scheduled each morning to further solidify their rather tenuous hold on relationships.

As I continue to do workshops, clinics and festivals around the country, I am increasingly aware that many of you who are reading this are experiencing difficulty in attracting and keeping young people in a youth choir. A part of that difficulty is, I believe, "the times." Statistics about drug use, runaways, pregnancy, truancy, and suicide could be quoted, but we are surely aware of these problems. This is not to despair over the state of today's youth. But, it is important to observe that there is increasing *pressure* on these young people in the choices they make. I am not now, nor have I ever been, negative about young people. I still believe in the power of youth properly motivated. This is what this book is about. I still believe in the power of worthy texts set to well-crafted music to attract and hold their interest. I still believe in a wide range and variety of musical styles and in the *response* of these over-scheduled, harried folks we call teenagers *to* that variety. They *can* and *do* respond to the challenge of leadership. They *will* care for each other and contribute to the good of the group. They *do* respond, but I find the whole process harder to accomplish! In talking with others of you across the country, I find I am not alone. This publication is a revision of earlier material. The ideas are partly mine and partly gleaned from many others—often from the youth themselves. It does not claim to be "everything-you-ever-wanted-to-know-about-youth-choir-work." What *is* here works. Take the ideas that seem valuable and refine them for your situation.

I am grateful for the years of ministry with Bob Carlisle, Don and Jane Vickburg, Jim Colclazier, Randy Hengst and Debbie Kuykendall in Norman, Oklahoma, and Tom Buckley, Boo Owens and Joe Pool in Dallas. They, along with youth themselves, taught me much. I am grateful to my friends John Erickson and Joe Sher, whose encouragement made possible the initial volume, and to my wife, Diane, who saw me through these experiences . . . and still does.

I GETTING STARTED

How do you attract youth to a church choir and keep them active and vital? It requires a belief on the part of the director that young people will respond to specific goals and can give responsible service on a regular basis if challenged to do so. In the beginning a short-range goal, such as performance of a specific work chosen for its obvious appeal, can attract. Adding responsibility for something specific, whether regular leadership in worship, a work project benefiting the community, singing for rest homes and hospitals, or a tour or trip, increases the potential for success. Outfits or robes strengthen identity and give the youth a group pride and a feeling of belonging to a worthwhile endeavor. Once challenged to service, they will seldom disappoint.

A Credo for Youth Choir Directors
I believe that young people will respond to
1. *Specific goals:* Worship leadership (on a regular basis), community music-making, mission projects, trips or tours.
2. *A varied musical diet:* Music of the Renaissance, Baroque, and Classical periods, folk music, selected rock style.
3. *The challenge of leadership:* Here, peer pressure can work to advantage; they govern—set and enforce standards within the group.
4. *Individual nurturing:* They need to feel someone's interest in them; they must "buy" your course of action for the choir.
I believe in young people, for they will rise to the highest expectation put before them.

Getting Down to Specifics
(a) The first short-range goal needs to be carefully chosen and publicized. A project with a definite date and place for performance can bring them out, such as a musical (more about that later) or a special service of anthems and hymns. They need the immediate challenge of service and responsibility.
(b) Find out who the "leaders" are and personally recruit them. A notice in the church newspaper or bulletin or a vague announcement at youth events will not bring in the troops. Find out who the responsible, popular young people are and target them. I have a "hit list" every summer of those who do not sing but are

potential leaders. I send notes, speak to them in the hall, and also encourage the present choir members to "get on their case"—all in a low key but persistent manner. I don't succeed in every instance, but the success rate is high. Young people need to be needed. Recruit the boys; if you get the boys, you can get the girls. If they say, "I can't sing," offer your help. Make them an offer they can't refuse: "If you'll come, I'll help you with the singing."

(c) Work to establish a good choral sound. Give them a varied musical diet.

(d) From the beginning, work on the group dynamic. These days, caring and concern for one's group members needs intentional nurture. Involve the young people in the process, helping them learn responsibility for *all* the others in the group. In Dallas, our wide age span (grades 7-12) made this imperative.

(e) Be there when they need you. They don't want or need a "pal." They have pals. You *can* function, however, where a parent often can't. That is to say, they may sometimes talk to you because it is easier. After all, you don't have to live together. You are safer, particularly if they trust you.

(f) Get as many as possible into voice classes where you can work with them on an individual basis. Relationships formed here may last for years, and through this experience the group is strengthened vocally and spiritually.

(g) Stick with your program! Don't give up! By all means, do not sell the young people short. Just at the time when all may seem to be lost, they will come through!

Worship Leadership

Responsibility and commitment are important words. I think it a good thing for a youth choir to sing *every* Sunday if possible. This forces them to prepare music and encourages their faithful commitment to the group. Identity coming from a sense of being part of the group (which can be depended upon to give regular, responsible leadership) grows as they serve. A trip or tour as a reward at the *end* of the year only makes sense as they have "labored in the vineyard" *during* the year.

Musical Variety

Although they are among the most conservative creatures abounding, youth can accept the challenges of responsible service and of appropriating the wide range of musical styles available. One cannot expect *equal* enthusiasm at first for all the elements in this varied diet, but Bach, Schütz, Handel, Mozart, etc., can be *sung* and *enjoyed*, as well as folk and rock literature with its more obvious appeal. We are often afraid that youth will not come unless we do contemporary music in the idiom of radio and TV. We are afraid that strict attendance regulations will keep them away. We are afraid that unless we ourselves are "with it" (or whatever is the current term) they will not like us or the choir. The truth is that we are often afraid to expect enough, and thus settle for a great deal less than they are ready to offer.

Leadership

It is important to trust in the ability of youth to govern. Officers and section leaders in a choir council can set attendance standards, assist in recruiting, plan work projects and aid the director in maintaining the high purpose for which the choir exists. When one has faith in the responsible judgment of these youth, seeks their counsel, expects high standards, and allows their assistance in administration, the choir program is strengthened and youth leadership skills developed. Enlisting their aid helps ensure success, as they begin to feel that it is *their* group and are charged with its nurture and care.

Unity of Approach

One also need recognize that these same youth who sing in the choir also attend church school and youth fellowship and participate in retreats, trail hikes, starv-a-thons and the like. Coordination with the youth director or Christian education director is essential. Sometimes either the choir person or the youth person may not realize that scheduling and working together make possible a host of useful activities for *all* the youth. Often, one "rejoices not" in the success of the other, but sees that success as a threat. I have been blessed with co-workers who made sure that youth were not scheduled for retreats on the weekend of an important choir program or rehearsal. Likewise, I have tried to be involved in the overall planning so that if rehearsals conflicted with a retreat weekend, a service project, or a total youth event, I gladly adjusted the choir schedule. A unified approach to planning serves the total program and enables youth participation in many activities without constant schedule conflicts. In the same way that trust between choir and director must be nurtured, so respect and appreciation for the efforts of one's co-worker(s) should be practiced. Neither the choir nor the youth department should be at war with the

11

other; rather, both should undergird and sustain the common effort of preaching and living the Gospel.

Age Groupings

A final consideration (after recruiting youth, establishing goals, expecting responsibility, trusting their leadership, and nurturing staff unity) is age grouping. Each situation is unique and no one pattern will suffice. My preference is for seventh and eighth grade or sixth through eighth grade in one group and ninth grade through twelfth in the other. If there are enough youth available to have two choirs, this allows more attention to changing voices in the younger grades and is a better social division as well. Because of numbers, many groups must involve seventh through twelfth grades, or sixth through twelfth, or seventh through college age, in order to have enough singers. Some programs keep youth in a children's choir until voice change, then move them up immediately into the next choir.

After considering availability of voices, current patterns of grouping in public school, age groupings in church school, or the needs of a particular church or community, the decision must be made: which pattern and which ages will work best together? We should always be creative and flexible, allowing the needs of a particular year to dictate. Don't get locked into one way of doing things; on the other hand, don't change the schedule from year to year either. Young people are creatures of habit and love the predictability of a good event in their midst. Find out what works for you and for them and stay with it as long as it works.

2   ESTABLISHING A SOUND

There are three factors in learning to play any instrument well:

1) How you hold your instrument

2) How you make a sound on that instrument

3) How the sound *sounds*

Think of the beginning violinist, for example. This budding Heifetz must learn what seems at first an awkward position for holding the instrument. Subsequently, as sounds begin to be made, family members find outside employment and neighbors sell houses to escape the scratching and whining of beginning bow on cheap cat gut. Finally, as progress is made with these first two factors, the sound becomes more pleasurable, even enjoyable. Any instrument requires a period of adjustment before the sound *sounds* good. There is no "magic" to developing good tone—no mysterious method, no incantation.

Establishing a choral "instrument" requires the same process with two important considerations. First, we come equipped with an "instrument" and use it from childhood in many ways not conducive to good singing. Local speech habits and patterns make the task even more difficult. Second, much of singing is not "natural": breathing is different, the body is held differently, word sounds are approached differently than in speech, and several parts or registers must be melded to form "one voice."

Even though the voice is controlled by the brain, the singing process is not within the realm of conscious control. One cannot simply "think a beautiful tone" and get it. Neither magic nor prayer, neither thinking nor wishing will produce good singing. We must instill "habitual" traits rather than calling on "naturalness," for much of what we do must be *learned*, gradually *becoming* natural. Training rooted in basic principles and vocal understanding is the route to beautiful tone. Much of what eventually feels "natural" is a habit made routine. Though these phrases are often used, you cannot actually do any of the following:

1) Place your voice in the "masque"
2) Put your hand on your diaphragm
3) Trap some sound behind your nose
5) Feel a light bulb in your throat
4) Sing through your eyes

Scientists say there is no such thing as voice placement. The larynx cannot be transplanted, nor can the air column be directed into the head, chest, or masque; vibrations originate in the larynx and resonate in the laryngeal and oral pharynxes and in the mouth.[1]

Should all imagery thus be thrown out? Not at all! Rather, imagery should be based on correct physical concepts of vocal function, allowing good singing *habits* to develop. Fact frees one to be imaginative and to take advantage of the pitches and speech timbres felt in different parts of the neck, mouth, and head. Imagery should be used "to suggest indirectly, through its psychological effects, a certain muscular setting which is awkward for the beginner."[2]

"It is not that fancy, in the form of the voice teacher's manifold imagery is to be condemned, but it must be known to be imagery, valuable and varied though it is. The teacher using it should bear in mind at all times the true facts, because when imagery becomes so vivid that it is transferred into the physical field and used to explain physiologic and acoustic phenomena, it becomes extremely dubious, unreliable, and even false. It is this misuse which is largely responsible for the bitter controversies over vocal methods, as well as for their often comical explanations. Furthermore, since imagery is largely individual and thus variable, when it is trusted as a physical explanation, the so-called true method becomes as variable as the individual temperament, instead of as stable as truth is usually expected to be."[3]

Many are the private voice students or chorus members who wail, "I've never done it this way before," to which the teacher replies, "I know." Good vocal habits must persistently be practiced by the student or group. "Natural" is a relative term. "Habitual" serves better as a definition. Singing is a process of learning effective posture, maximizing breath and developing resonance. We simply must not teach by sensation alone, nor expect our singers to produce good tone automatically or "naturally." Singers should be asked to do those things they *can* do, and not be frustrated with meaningless injunctions to place or feel something in a certain part of the head. Remember the young choral director who, after exhorting his flock to "blend, blend," was met with the reply, "We would be delighted to blend if you would tell us *where, when,* and *with whom.*" Allowing for over-simplification, the three factors of good tone are:

1) Holding the instrument
2) Making a sound on that instrument
3) Developing the traits which help that instrument *sound* good

Holding the Instrument

Realizing that any instrument requires explanation and practice in the mechanics of use, singers should be asked to hold their rib cage (not chest) up, keep shoulders down, and allow breath to flow in, feeling expansion below the rib cage, at the sides, and in the back. This movement of air causes bodily expansion because the air is moving, not because of a muscular action pushing it. The rib cage and shoulders want "naturally" to slump when breath leaves the body, and singers must be trained to hold the rib cage up, letting the flow of breath do the work.

Making a Sound

The action of taking a "cold air" breath, feeling this cold air in the back of the throat where the uvula is located, works better than any injunction I know to open the throat:

> If the various tricks of the trade that voice teachers use to improve quality are analyzed, most or all of them will be found to be devices for directly or indirectly enlarging the throat.

15

The teacher may not be aware of this, but simply knows that such devices get results. Thus, the proper taking in of breath will often loosen the interfering muscles, the jaw relaxing more and more the deeper the breath. The feeling of the beginning of a natural yawn, or the relaxation felt after its completion, are aids to securing a large throat.[4]

Once the body is held in proper position and the breath is taken with a relaxed or open throat, the sequence is:

THINK (pitch) . . . BREATHE and SING

The taking of breath implies completion in a sound, setting the voice in motion. This concept is the origin of the phrase "singing on the breath." Breath should never be held and the voice should never be struck, belted, started, jarred, or forced. Singing should always be allowed to flow "naturally," keeping in mind that establishing good vocal habits will bring this about.

Developing "Sound" Traits

Correct stance, open throat, and coordination of breath with tone to set the voice singing all work toward better and better sound. Thus when a choir sounds good it is no accident, nor is magic involved. Rather, persistence from the director based on vocal knowledge is the key. I commend study of the publications listed in the bibliography and auditing of voice studio work, choir rehearsals, recordings, and public performances to give a frame of reference for sound and a renewed dedication to its pursuit.

Endnotes

[1] Stanley, *The Science of Voice*, Chapter 4, pp. 39-40
[2] Stanley, 39-40
[3] Stanley, 39-40
[4] Bartholomew, Wilmer T., "The Role of Imagery in Voice Teaching," as reprinted from the 1935 Volume of Proceedings, the Music Teachers National Association, pp. 15-16.

3   PRACTICAL APPLICATION

In actual practice, how can one deal with the essentials of posture, tall vowel sounds, warming-up and tuning-up? The choir will take the easy way out in most cases and, unless one persists, the results will always be less than satisfactory. No one wants to sing in a bad choir but if the director offers unexciting literature, accepts poor posture and permits inattention to vowel sounds or tuning, singers will never grow. Some will drop out, others will cause constant discipline problems, and the goal of a fine singing organization will never be realized. Let us consider the following:

Posture
Ask the singers to raise both arms high above the head, find the rib cage with one hand, then bring the other arm down, leaving rib cage high and shoulders relaxed. This is the correct stance for singing. Encouraging this stance on a continuing basis means using *terminology that does not sound like nagging.* "Sit up straight," can sound much like "pick up your socks," "mow the yard," or "take out the trash," if one is not careful. Sit up straight they must, however, and they are encouraged to do so by statements such as: "when you sit down, sit up," "move your back away from the chair," "plant both feet firmly on the floor," "no good singer sits with crossed legs," and "stand up from your waist." Anthems and hymnals must be held up so that chins are not squashing the vocal mechanism and so that sound is coming *out*, not *down*. Learning anthems with copies casually laid in laps or with elbows on legs in a slumped position does not bring results. My stock phrase is, *"where your music is, there will your eyes be also."* Positive encouragement of posture is a constant but rewarding task.

Tall Vowel Sounds
Vowel sounds are formed in the *back* and shaped in the *front.* Often singers *think* they are opening mouths wide and are amazed when they cannot even get two fingers in that opening. Ask them to place their fingers (at least two) vertically in the mouth to check this. Ask them to place their fingers directly behind the ear lobes and feel the action of the jaw when it drops. This does not feel "natural" at first but must be learned. Relaxing the jaw and standing each sound tall in the back of the mouth creates more sound,

17

blend, and beauty, since all voices sing the *same sound* at the same time.

Warm-up, Tune-up

A five-minute warm-up and tune-up period says, "we now come together as a group—an ensemble—to review the basics of posture and tall vowel sounds and immediately apply what we are learning to the literature of the moment." It is "Christian" to sound good, to sing in tune with proper balance and blend, with well-formed, tall vowel sounds, and to allow the words we sing to flow through us to those who hear. This worthy goal cannot be accomplished without technique.

Many do not warm up because they feel it a waste of time. If warm-ups *are* attempted, they are often too complicated and have little or no application to the music to be sung. One could get up every day for a year and sing *"mah, may, mee, moh, moo"* like a magic incantation, but nothing vocally productive would happen. One would be better off with simple exercises that lead immediately into application. Developing a *sound in the room* as a frame of reference is preferable to "mah-ing" or "mee-ing" while scurrying up and down the scale in a meaningless effort. Even in a workshop situation where time is of the essence, if a basic sound and co-operation with posture, open mouths, tall vowel sounds, etc., is not established, nothing of musical worth can be accomplished.

The results will be gradual, but building on a solid foundation will produce long-term results. We are tempted to forego the basics in a rush to learn anthems and prepare programs, but sooner or later we must deal with "how it sounds."

Warming Up

I. Begin with loosening up the body
    A. Everyone stands, stretches tall (arms over head).
    B. Bring arms down, leave rib cage *high,* shoulders *down.*
    C. Gently drop head on chest, roll clockwise and counter-clockwise, *letting jaw drop open.*
    D. Roll shoulders forward and backward.
    E. Clasp hands, stretch toward the front, then toward the back.
    F. Bend over, "hang loose," straighten up gradually, letting back pull you up.
    G. *Occasionally,* turn to neighbor and give a quick back-rub; turn back other way.

II. Get the breath going
   A. Ask everyone to take a *cold air breath* (no audible noise).
   B. *Feel* cold air in the back of the throat in a lifting sensation.
   C. Take breath, blow breath out *slowly*, keeping *body tall— don't cave in.*
   D. Blow out an imaginary candle with a *"sss"* sound *from the body*—do five in a row.
   E. Blow *steadily* with a *"sss"* sound for certain number of counts.
III. Get the tone going
   A. In the example below, ask for a "yawny" feeling (not muffled, however) with plenty of space *inside* the mouth, going immediately to the *"Mmmm"* with lips *lightly* together. The sound is *Yahmmmmm*. Feel the cold air breath as you inhale, feel the lifting sensation, close your lips over the tall *"AH"* shape to *"Mmmm."*

   Ask the singers to slide the pitches in a continuous tone— liken it to an elevator going up and down while the elevator shaft stays the same—don't cave in the throat as you go— keep the hummy sound going. Move the exercise up by half steps.

   This is wonderful for both warming up the voice and for developing flexibility. If the tone is constantly moving on a resonant sound (*"Mmmm"*) with plenty of space inside and the body is in singing position, the chances for tension to set in are minimized. You may find that singers have trouble "sliding" at first, but encourage them to sing continuously. Ask them to "take all the stops along the way, not the express route." Cushion the sound at the bottom with air, don't let it "bottom out."

Yahm

B. Using the five-note descending pattern below, you may try some of the following, continuing to work on a lifting sensation when breath is taken, and coordination of breath with tone, relaxed jaw, and feeling of space inside the mouth:

YAHmmm	YAHmmm	YAHmmm	YAHmmm	YAHmmm
YAHmmmee	YAHmmmee	YAHmmmee	YAHmmmee	YAHmmmee
Voommm	Voommm	Voommm	Voommm	Voommm
Zoommm	Zoommm	Zoommm	Zoommm	Zoommm

For YAHmmmee, be careful that the "EE" has a tall shape, (not too smiley)
For *Voommm, Zoommm,* use lots of "V" or "Z" consonant sound, tall "OO" sound.

IV. *Tuning the group*
   A. Begin as shown in example on octave "A" with a tall "OO" sound.
   B. Everyone sustains (take a breath when necessary) while basses move slowly down the scale, *listening.*
   C. Altos move to third of chord, *everyone listening for tuning and balance.*

After this initial experience, ask everyone to sing the octave "A" on *"loo"* again, while holding your hand horizontally. As you move your hand to a vertical position ask the singers to stand the sound tall inside their mouths *without forcing for more sound.* Usually,

20

a dramatic difference will be apparent. Ask the girls to stand the sound tall while the boys listen; then turn the procedure around. Do the simple warm-up again, this time with a better sound on *"loo."* Encourage the singers to take a cold air breath and to sing with this feeling, remembering the sequence: *think* (hear the pitch)—*breathe and sing.* With a well-formed vowel sound and a tuned chord, move the entire chord up and down by half-steps, listening for balance and blend. *"OO"* is the reference vowel and can be the model for other vowel sounds. Start with a *tall "loo"* sound on the four-part chord established and begin to work the well-formed, well-shaped *"loo"* sound into other vowel sounds as follows:

LOO .....LOH .....LOO
LOO .....LAY ......LOO
LOO .....LEE ......LOO
LOO .....LAH .....LOO

Changes in This Routine

1. Begin by tuning the D Major (or subsequent chord) up from the bass.
2. Sing the four-part chord staccato on *"doot"* using the following pattern:

3. Tuning in case of few tenors:

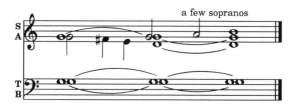

Breathiness

Breathiness in young voices is always a problem and the use of *"M"* and *"N"* as resonance-producers gives "ping" to the sound.

Using the same four-part vocalises, substitute *"moo"* or *"noo"* for *"loo"* and work for a "hummy" feeling before opening to the vowel. Ask the singers to put both hands lightly on the cheek bones under the eye sockets and feel the resonant sensation or tingle. Encourage them to keep the vowel tall as they open from *"M"* or *"N"* and to have some of that resonant sensation present at all times. Our aim is to *add resonance*, not *encourage nasality*, and vowel shape must be *tall* as resonance is added.

Another technique for eliminating breathiness and tightness is what William Vennard calls the *"yawn-sigh"*:

> This exercise is quite informal, and should be done as easily and comfortably as possible. It consists of simulating a yawn and exhaling gently and vocally. The emotional atmosphere should be happy, relieved. The mood should be of relaxation, like the feeling at the end of a perfect day, tired but happy. Have the students imagine they are sitting in an easy chair and have just put on their slippers; they stretch and say ah-h-h-h-h, what a day! The sound should begin with an imaginary *"H."*
>
> In order to get the desired relaxation without breathiness, it will be necessary that head tone or quasi-falsetto be used. The initial pitch should not be a definite one, but it should be one that is comfortably located in the upper part of the range and should then glide down into the chest voice. What is desired is a light, clear, heady voice, the heaviness of which can be increased at will as the pitch descends. The yawn-sigh is an exercise for freedom . . . which can be either loud or soft, though it is usually *piano* to *mezzo-forte*.
>
> Application of this private voice technique within a large group initially brings a combination of hesitancy and silliness, but, gradually, voices begin to relax and open up. Do the yawn-sigh in three steps:

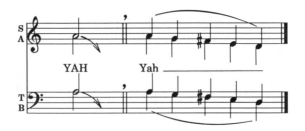

1. Ask for a sound (a sigh) from everyone in the room.
2. Put this sigh on a pitch, asking everyone to slide the pitch down, with jaw relaxed and loose.
3. Follow the "slide" by singing down a five-note scale pattern with the same relaxed feeling.[5]

Still another technique for eliminating breathiness is *staccato singing* using *"doot"* or *"pahn"* on well-known hymns, such as *Come, Thou Almighty King (Italian Hymn), All People That on Earth Do Dwell (Old 100th), I'll Praise My Maker (Old 113th),* or *Ye Watchers and Ye Holy Ones (Lasst uns erfreuen).* Hymns with limited range work best.

Warm-up Variations

Learning to *sound* better involves *repetition* and *variation.* The director who understands what he or she is after will devise new, sometimes novel ways to get at the basic problem of voice building. Our job should be to get a good *vocal attack on the breath* (a cold air breath) with *vowel quality, range,* and *beauty.* Sometimes it is educationally sound not to come head-on at the group but to involve them before they know what is happening. I share the following variation, therefore, as an idea of humor for a good vocal purpose.

On a recent excursion down the Guadalupe River in Texas, we both floated the river and went "toobing" in a nearby facility. For the uninformed, one hops on a large inflated tube and alternately floats and swirls down part of the river. It is great fun! Upon arriving at the place to rent the tubes, I noticed the sign "Toobs for rent"—and thus was born a set of "Toobing warm-ups." Pronounciation of *bing* should be *beeng.* Work the *"OO"* sound into a tall *"EE"* sound, careful that the *"EE"* not become shallow. They love *"GWAH-DAH-LOOP"* and it accomplishes a good purpose. (Begin in C major—move up by half steps.)

TOO - bing, TOO - bing, TOO - bing, TOO - bing, TOO - bing.

ROW - ing, ROW - ing, ROW - ing, ROW - ing,

RAP - id - ly RAP - id - ly ROW - ing.

SHOOT - ing, SHOOT - ing, SHOOT - ing, SHOOT - ing,

SHOOT - ting the loop.

GWAH-DAH - LOO - (p)
(Guadalupe)

Another warm-up variation young people enjoy is, MAH, MAH, KEE-LAH, BLIP-BLIP.

1. Basses and tenors begin on **A**

2. Altos join on **B**

3. Sopranos join on **C**

4. Any variation is possible. It needs to be done with great energy, moving the key up and down, and changing around so that everyone gets to sing every part. It also is excellent for tongue and teeth movement.

Variations Using Anthem Literature or Hymns

The use of hymns for eliminating breathiness has already been mentioned. Sections of hymns may be used as well for warm-up purposes. Here are a few suggestions:

1) *Come, Christians, Join to Sing (Spanish Hymn)*

Using only the first line, good attack on "come" and well-shaped "alleluia" with a feeling of singing over the top of the phrase.

2) *All Creatures of Our God and King (Lasst uns erfreuen)*

The first stanza of this is good for negotiating the skip from "and with us sing" to "alleluia." Ask singers to feel that they sing *down* when they go for higher pitches. Feeling *sideways* instead of *up* may be helpful.

3) *Come, Thou Almighty King (Italian Hymn)*

Excellent for that well-inspirited lift of *cold air,* good consonant sound on "come" and working upward in range. Use only the first three measures.

Anthem Literature

It is useful to use sections of an anthem you are rehearsing for vocal/warm-up purposes. Look for places where the choir seems to be having trouble vocally and incorporate them into your warm-up. Some examples:

1) *For the Beauty of the Earth*—John Rutter (Hinshaw HMC 133)

Begin in B♭, singing only "for the beauty of the earth." Move the exercise up by half steps. Emphasize continuous vocal line as you move upward and a relaxed vowel sound on "earth."

2) *Gather the People*—Stan Pethel (Hope GC 861)

The first three words: "gather the people" when sung, have a tendency to be shallow, forced and throaty on the *"ee"* vowel sound. Begin lower, work for relaxed *"ee"* vowel, good explosion on consonant *"p"* and a connection between the first three notes (gath-er the) and the last two (peo-ple). It takes more energy to ascend than to descend. Work for the idea of singing "across the phrase," "through the phrase," "over the top," feeling downward as you sing over the phrase.

3) *I Know That My Redeemer Lives*—Gilbert Martin (Beckenhorst BP 1269)

Begin "I know" with a good *"Nnnn"* on "know" and carry that up the phrase. Expand the vowel on the word "what" so that the whole line makes sense: I know that my redeemer lives, what joy the blest assurance gives.

Normally, I don't recommend printed vocalises because they are often too difficult. You know best what your group needs and should devise ways to help them along. The simple ones are always the best ones, for then concentration can center on what is happening vocally, not on something cute, a difficult rhythm, or wide range. An exception to the above is the collection entitled *Sing Legato* by Dr. Kenneth Jennings, published by Neil A. Kjos. There is a choral edition (V74) and an accompaniment edition (V74A). These are, I think, excellent and worth doing.

Applying the Warm-up to Anthem Literature

In the warm-up segment of the rehearsal, attention is drawn to good posture, tall vowel sounds, tuning and balance of three and four-part chords, and the beginning of a vocal attack which is on-the-breath. The beginnings of ensemble and the slow but steady process of voice building are here established, enabling the choir to sing anthems and hymns with beauty, clarity, and understanding. *The first anthem or hymn chosen after the warm-up is crucial, and a piece well along in the learning process or a well-known hymn works best so that concentration on warm-up techniques is fostered.* As an example, let us take *The Gift of Love,* an arrangement of a folk tune by Hal Hopson (Hope CF 148).

Notice the outline of the tune. Range is good for everyone (D-d); the tune is beautiful and easily learned. Work immediately for the tall *"loo"* sound just sung in the warm-up and for an attack

27

From *The Gift of Love*, arr. Hal H. Hopson. Copyright © 1972 by Hope Publishing Co., Carol Stream, IL 60188. All rights reserved. Used by permission.

on-the-breath. Encourage an attack which allows the breath to lead
into singing, taking care that resonance or a "hummy" feeling is
also present.

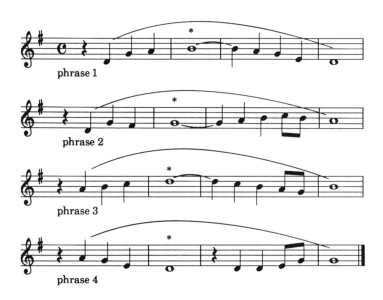

phrase 1

phrase 2

phrase 3

phrase 4

   No doubt, the choir will lose energy and tonal beauty each time
at the top of the phrase, and here is a chance to encourage intensity
by using a musical concept: *the top of the phrase.* The overall
destination of each of the four phrases looks like an arc or half-
circle and singers must *pull* toward the longer note, sing *through*
it, and let the phrase relax on the other side. Musical laws are
physical laws and it takes more energy to ascend than to descend.
Encourage them by conducting the arc of the phrase or drawing
an arc on the chalkboard as each phrase is sung, encouraging
singing *through* the long note. In addition to this valuable concept
in musical energy, ask the choir to read aloud the text:
      Though I may *SPEAK* with bravest fire,
      And have the *GIFT* to all inspire
      And have not *LOVE*, my words are vain
      As sounding *BRASS*, or hopeless gain.
In order for this *text* to have meaning, the musical energy must
carry the thought along, particularly where the long note at the

top of the phrase is concerned. If the musical energy dies, the text loses all meaning.

Finally, deal with the overall concept of a four-phrase structure which looks like the following:

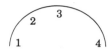

Looking for relationships between phrases is another brick in our building of good tone, musicality, and text understanding. The total approach is one which engages one ingredient of the piece, either tune or text, at a time. Seldom is the piece "read through." Learning is strengthened if one aspect is accomplished at a time, always keeping in mind the musical whole. It is never possible simply to learn the "right notes" and add the "music" later. Shape, style, tone, text meaning, and word shape must all be a part of the process as we learn.

Endnotes

[5] Vennard, William. *Singing, The Mechanism and the Technique*, Carl Fischer, revised edition, 1964, p. 128.

4   CHOOSING THE MUSIC

In my experience, youth choirs sound good on a variety of musical styles. This variety, in itself, is an important ingredient in keeping and sustaining interest throughout the year. There are three style-types that seem to work particularly well: 1) late-Renaissance, Baroque, Classical; 2) Folk; and 3) Rock. As I discuss these three style-types and illustrate with musical examples, you will understand that I am stating the case for a desired sound and articulation rather than attempting to uphold the canons of historical accuracy. Music exists in sound, not in a printed description in a textbook. Our ears, combined with historical knowledge, should always be our guide.

Music of the first style-type (late-Renaissance, Baroque, Classical) has in common a sound and articulation emphasizing lightness of texture, crisp consonants, upbeat articulation and a rhythmic drive with energy and life—not volume—as the sound source. Anthems such as *Cantate Domino* (Pitoni), *Sing a New Song* (Schütz/Jennings), *Keep Me Faithfully in Thy Paths* (Handel/Proulx), and *Praise the Lord* (Mozart/Hopson) all have this common sound idea. (Specific information on all anthems mentioned may be found in the repertoire listing in the index.) Young voices sound good in this style-type because those voices are already light (or *should* be!) and because anything rhythmic is easily executed. Only when we grow older does our natural rhythmic sense slow down and we experience difficulty with light, energetic music, especially that containing syncopation. Youth live in a rhythmically musical world and they naturally accommodate to this style.

In teaching a piece like *Sing a New Song* the approach may begin instrumentally with choir singing on a neutral vowel *(doot or pahm)*, emphasizing clarity of pitch and crispness of rhythm.

The sound ideal is that of a recorder consort with a bit of "chiff" or air in the vocal attack. After this sound is well established by rehearsing on a neutral syllable, text may then be spoken in a crisp, well-articulated manner with attention to rise and fall of individual words:

Sing ă nĕw | sŏng tŏ | Gŏd thĕ | Lŏrd
Sing and give | praise with | one ac-|cord

Sing a new song to God the Lord.

Sing and give praise with one ac - cord.

From *Sing a New Song,* Schütz/Jennings. Copyright © 1975 Belwin-Mills Publishing Corp. c/o CPP/Belwin, Inc., Miami, FL 30014. International copyright secured. Made in USA. All rights reserved. Used by permission.

When we ask choirs to speak a text we should insist on a light sound from them in a mid-range vocally. Musicality of text must be our goal. The intent here is that shorter notes pull toward longer notes, not in an over-accented manner, but more *poco-staccato* to *poco-tenuto*, with direction *across* the bar lines. Note also how the arranger, Carolyn Jennings, has caught the real flavor and rhythmic interest of the piece, scoring accompaniment for flute and string bass. The staccato markings for the quarter notes in both flute and string bass illustrate my point of shorter notes pulling toward longer notes. This arrangement is also a good example of letting your ear be your guide. It is, in my opinion, one of the best anthems in print for either youth or adult choirs.

In teaching *Keep Me Faithfully in Thy Paths,* one may begin with interest in the upbeat or anacrusic nature of the piece. The two quarter notes at the beginning are sung lighter, *poco-staccato* and *across* the bar line to the dotted quarter, with a lift on the word "faithfully" rather than a strong "down-beat." Direction in this music is critical, particularly through the word "thy" to the word "paths." The first page of the anthem is reproduced and marked with accents and an arrow to show destination. Note the semi-bar lines at measures 8 and 11, reminiscent of Gregorian chant notation. These denote phrase endings where a lift should occur before going on. The time involved to shape the phrase is the time it takes to breathe easily (with no sound) before starting the second phrase. The breath comes after "Lord" and before "in." If one begins with a clear intent to influence the articulation *and* the direction, one finds that right sound which is light, clear, never heavy, and the young people learn *both* style *and* correct pitches. It is always a good rehearsal technique to sing on a neutral syllable, as mentioned earlier, with energetic sound and attention to artic- ulation *and* direction.

In my judgment, the same ideas regarding articulation, sound, and direction found in the Schütz piece and the Handel anthem apply to the Mozart *Praise the Lord.* This is courtly, dance-like music with a string quartet as a basic frame of reference for sound. One learns to look for many changes and short phrases in this music. It remains "poised in the center, ready to move in any direction" to quote Alice Parker in *Creative Hymn Singing.* On a word chart, the text/articulation would look like the following:

KEEP ME FAITHFULLY IN THY PATHS

TWO MIXED VOICES AND ORGAN

From the First Chandos Anthem, c. 1717

George Frederick Handel, 1685-1759
Edited by Richard Proulx

‾ ˘ • • ´ ˘
Praise the Lord, be Joy-ful
‾ ˘ • • ´ ˘
Praise the Lord, be Joy-ful

The first page of this anthem is reproduced with accents marked in the music. With every piece in this general style category, an approach emphasizing energy, well-formed vowel sounds, crisp articulation and the enjoyment of the dance-like, moving rhythms, makes for an exciting experience for young people, with integrity, maintaining what—in your best judgment—the composer intended. To absorb this style flavor, listen to good recordings or go to live performances. Listen for those which employ lightness, clarity, and well-directed energy. Young people may not leave the first rehearsal with obvious enthusiasm over their initial encounter with Heinrich, Johann, Wolfgang or Franz, but they eventually get caught up in this style and never tire of the diet. What they work hardest to accomplish, they eventually enjoy the most. On the tour bus (more of that in a later chapter) you can look for these pieces, particularly those unaccompanied, to be the favorites sung. It *is* worth the effort.

Music of the second style period (folk) is represented by anthems such as *On Eagles' Wings* (Joncas), *Advent Prayer* and *Prayer for Guidance* (Pote), *In Thee, Do I Put My Trust* (Beebe), *Walk Along Beside Me* (Besig), and *Kum Bah Yah* (arr. Lojeski). This sound ideal or quality is almost built in. Youth respond with a natural authentic singing which suits this music perfectly. One still works for beautiful vowel sounds, good breath connection, support, phrasing, and vocal line, but, unlike singers with more mature voices who often sing rather heavily in this style, these youthful artists inherently sing with the appropriate sound and quality. What they do not accomplish inherently, however, is phrasing and direction. Phrases should have a relationship one to another, and this must be taught. In *On Eagles' Wings,* for instance, it would be possible to sing all four phrases the same, but consider what happens when the first phrase acts as introductory to the overall phrase structure, the second phrase is sung stronger with an urging toward the third and biggest phrase, followed by a tapering off for phrase four. A simple diagram illustrates this basic point:

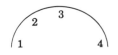

Praise the Lord, Be Joyful!

from *Litaniae de venerabilialtaris sacramento*
SATB accompanied

Paraphrased from Psalm 100
by Hal H. Hopson

Wolfgang Amadeus Mozart (1756-1791)
Arranged by Hal H. Hopson

REFRAIN

Young people inherently use the appropriate *sound* for this second style type, but must be taught relationship *and* direction.

Another example is the beautiful *Advent Prayer* in which we want the choir to understand both the *relationship* of the four-phrase structure, and the *direction* over the bar line so that the individual phrases have line and flow. Bar lines are a notational convention and should never stop vocal line, in my opinion.

Music of the third style period (rock) is probably the most basic to those with whom we work in youth choirs. Anthems like *Gather the People* (Pethel), *Sing Ye Joyfully* (Besig), *Amazing Grace* (arr. Coates), or musicals like *Creation* (Bobrowitz and Porter), *Reason to Rejoice* (Pote), and *Season to Celebrate* (Pote), call for a more energetic sound than either of the other styles discussed. The problem or challenge for the director is not the young people's *interest* in this style type, but their continued work on the elements of good choral singing: well-formed vowel sounds, proper posture, crisp consonants, and a non-forced sound. They will want to "sing out" with a *forced* sound if not nurtured in a *vibrant, energetic* sound. Many a director, after having carefully worked for appropriate tone in other literature, loses the battle as his or her group launches into a full-scale attack on a rock anthem. Electric guitar players and drummers, like enthusiastic pianists and organists, sometimes play too loudly which overstimulates the choral tone. Balance *is* possible and voices can remain fresh and vital, not diminishing the verve, life, and excitement of this style. But over-singing is never the answer. I am not advocating vocal anemia, just good vocal sense. It *is* possible!

The Pethel anthem, *Gather the People,* is a good example of the type of music young people love to sing—and often over-sing!

In teaching this anthem, it will be important to vocalize the first part of the first bar of text (Gather the people) because of the placement of the *"EE"* vowel on what is a pivot note for both the guys and the gals. If we begin to vocalize just the first six eighth notes in a lower key, D Major, for instance, asking for an energetic but noiseless cold air breath, exploding the *"p"* of "people" and encouraging a kind of vocal production that has the feeling of stepping into the higher note rather than attacking or "belting" it, we can, by raising the pitch a half-step at a time, arrive at the correct key of G Major with a much better sound. It may be that we will have to work on the *"ee"* vowel separately to keep it tall and sung with somewhat relaxed jaw. By working at a lower, more

An Advent Prayer

for Two-Part Mixed Voices, with Keyboard

Allen Pote

40

comfortable range, allowing breath to flow, psychologically approaching the upper note by singing *into* rather than reaching *for* it, exploding the consonant and freeing the vowel, we should have good sound *with* energy!

It is advantageous, secondly, to head for the most important words of the text, letting the others go:

> gather the PEO-ple, let the TRUM-pet SOUND (AH-oo)

> call out the CON-gre-GA-tions where they MAY be FOUND (AH-oo)

I am not advocating punching these important words, rather, energizing them with good consonant articulation and using energy instead of loud, boisterous, "un-thinking" singing. Often, I have been known to tell a group, "that was an unconsidered sound . . . let's try again." Those of us who have done this for a period of time know how difficult it is to keep this energy level up—breath flowing, bodies alert, jaws relaxed, concentration alive—and how easy it is to allow the choir to let loose and "holler" as we say in Texas. I encourage all who work with young people to continue to work for good vocal technique *regardless* of the literature. This approach will pay big dividends.

All types or styles of music can and must have exciting performance, but careful tonal work need not be sacrificed. Variety in musical diet is essential, not only for the congregation or audience, but for the choir as well. Music should live in its natural habitat and sound like what it is. The more difficult works have to be nurtured and brought along slowly, but a real pride of accomplishment, matched by a growing love of something well-crafted, from any period, can be developed. Once the choir has tasted the reward of a variety of musical styles, well performed, they will always want more.

5 STUDYING AND CONDUCTING YOUR CHOICES

"The truth is in the score" is always a beginning point for score study. In a graduate seminar several years ago, an aspiring conductor was leading choir and orchestra through a rather strange reading of a Mozart work. Stopped and asked to explain his interpretation, he responded: "I'm doing it this way because I *feel* it this way." The response from the instructor was: "We don't care how *you* feel it, how does Mozart feel it?" Our job, it seems to me, is to do our homework so that the initial exposure to the piece has a chance of eventually resulting in a good performance. If our choirs always attempt a "stylistic" performance of the music chosen, and if each piece lives in a healthy environment, speaking honestly through the choir to the congregation/audience with clarity and ease, our job is made easier. What then is a definition of "style" and how does one achieve a "stylistic" performance? What are the questions one should ask of a piece of music prior to its introduction? I'm glad you asked!

Style
Here is a very simple definition of style: style is the right *sound* for the music, *in the room*, taking into account the *performers* (singers, players) and being acutely aware of the following questions.

What is the background of the piece?
We should ask of an anthem what kind of piece it is, where it comes from, and if there are others similar. Is this piece typical or atypical as we are aware of the total output of this composer? Are there recordings available? In what other media has this composer written?

What considerations are there regarding text?
Choosing a text well set to music is essential. Dealing with musicality of the language itself, with awareness of individual word shapes and overall destination, bears much fruit. Nothing serves a "stylistic" performance as well as *speaking* a text to ascertain the above qualities. Each language has certain diction requirements that make singing different from speaking, but, in the main, the

43

way it is spoken, with correct word stress, is the way it is sung. Phrasing makes sense, enunciation makes sense, and the music makes sense when this approach is employed. Choirs may feel punished when asked to speak aloud a text, but if they will do so in a middle range vocally, listening to the rise and fall of word shapes and being aware of destinations, many other vocal and musical problems may be overcome. Awkwardness in text setting, clumsy prosody, false accents, all work against the life of the music. By the same token, a well-set text, sung without the articulation which musicality of language demands, usually results in a stale, unexciting, non-stylistic performance.

What about the edition or editing?

If an arrangement or transcription is chosen, what is the original scoring or accompaniment? This question opens up possibilities in organ registration, or in the use of other instruments such as guitar, cello or flute. If the original scoring is for string quartet, brass quintet, or solo flute, we are informed in our choice of organ registration or in utilizing our own local instrumentalists. An honest edition will always make the editor's judgments known in brackets or by written comment. We have a musical right to know if the original key has been changed, if dynamic markings are not original, if text has been altered or translated, or if the accompaniment has been simplified. Our musical choices related to style can and should be based on this knowledge.

What about tempo?

Where the piece will be heard, that is, the room or hall, makes a great difference in choice of tempi. Does this room lend itself to a faster or slower tempo? Do we ever rehearse fast pieces more slowly and vice versa? Often, a certain tempo is learned and then thought of as gospel, when a different pace may be required as the acoustics of the room or the limitations of the performers demand. This is one of the positive aspects of touring because flexibility of sound and tempo must be in relation to constant adjustment to new physical settings.

Because the famous Canadian pianist, Glenn Gould, *could* play the Bach preludes and fugues at some of his furious tempi does not mean they *sound* best at that speed. I question the judgment of a choir which "dashes off" a musical tour-de-force—one which makes its impact, not because the right questions were asked of the piece, the room, and the performers, but rather because the

44

choir simply sang at a faster speed or a louder dynamic than normally thought possible. We have all heard these types of performances. Because one has built up muscles, one does not need to flex them when asked for directions to the choir room—a simple gesture will suffice. The score is our only guide and it must speak while we try not to intrude with our own bias.

The Initial Exposure to the Music

The kind of thoughtful questioning advocated above allows for creative teaching and for establishing what I call the "want-to" in the choir. It makes that initial "brush" with a new piece successful. Because of our careful study, we make priority decisions about where to start and with what segment or section. Our striving, from the beginning, is for a musical approach including phrasing, dynamics, style, text stress, and beauty—all of which cannot be added *after* the correct notes are learned. Part of the process is to establish an overall idea of the musicality *and* style as learning unfolds.

Seldom in teaching a new piece do I simply read through it with a youth choir. I have found that a better approach is to begin with one important characteristic of the anthem: a melodic motive (such as the beginning phrase of *Gather the People),* a particular rhythmic section, or an interesting part of the text. I believe that a choir should always deal with text in several ways:

1) As a whole, for meaning
2) In phrases, for musicality, intelligibility, and form
3) For enjoyment of individual words and word sounds

Dealing with the musicality of the language, in this way, makes for sensitive, stylistic performances. There is a great range of articulation available but many choirs often sing everything pretty much the same—the same dynamic, the same rhythmic energy, and the same unmusical rendering of text. Words are our power and we should allow them to serve us better. It is not so much a matter of putting on powerful consonants, though consonant articulation is certainly important, but of understanding *where* the music is going. A well-set anthem is always easier to sing because its music and text go together. Our job as conductors is to understand *how* the piece goes together and educate our singers so that when they sing, they *know* where they are going.

Problem Areas: Diction

To advocate "singing as we speak" is not to endorse regionalism in singing, nor to suggest that work on vowel sounds and consonants is not essential. The concept of standing vowel sounds tall has been discussed, and the drilling in mechanics of vowels and consonants is always essential! I call this work "choral hygiene." Singers are notoriously hard to convince (double that statement as related to teenagers) that a vowel sound is not tall enough or a consonant not prominent enough. Words simply have to be broken up into dipthongs or tripthongs, and attention to the "least of these" promotes real understanding in the choir, allowing the music to speak. I commend study of books on diction and of the fine pamphlet, *A Musical Approach to Diction* by Dr. B. R. Henson (Hinshaw #HMC 133). Auditing of recordings, private vocal studio work, and live performances attunes us as can nothing else. In our study, we must be aware of the small details which come together to form the whole. On the other hand, what doth it profit a choir to have every *"t"* and *"AH-oo"* in place without musical intelligibility or style? Phrasing relationships and attention to musicality of text do much for clear diction. Phrases have a relationship to each other in a well-crafted anthem and finding and showing them gives life to the music and understanding to the listener. We must constantly balance the "scrub" work of vowels and consonants with artistic considerations of text, phrasing, and form.

46

Problem Areas: Form

Too often, the conductor does not have a good idea about *how* a particular anthem is constructed. The best advice to give, I believe, is that of proceeding from the overall structure toward smaller units. Another way of saying this is to start from the outside and work in, from the large form to smaller forms. Form also means looking for *change* in the music: change in *texture* (four voices to two voices to solo), change in *accompaniment* (interest shifting from choir to instrumental accompaniment), changes in *mood, sonority, speed*, changes from *staccato* to *legato*, from *loud* to *soft*, from *short phrase(s)* to *long phrase(s)*. When a composition is well studied by the conductor, the next step is to make the choir aware of these changes—to ask for them in rehearsal, then to listen to hear the result. Our study should never cause us to fool ourselves into imagining that what we hear in our inner ear is actually what is being sung. We should honestly audit our groups and creatively seek to speed their improvement. Often, a musical or tonal problem will be solved as aspects of form are revealed. The *how* and *why* are most important. We should always be careful not to *talk* our groups to death, however. In rehearsals with the Dallas Symphony Orchestra, Maestro Eduardo Mata often *sings* what he wants. That communication is powerful and, it should be stated, no one present has any doubt that the Maestro *knows* what he wants to hear. He *knows* the sound, the articulation, the pacing, the quality, and communicates them *because* of his study and experience. Singing is a wonderful tool which choral directors often eschew and substitute with too much verbal exchange. Mata also communicates by his *physical gestures*, his *conducting*.

47

Problem Areas: Conducting

Nothing is quite so ludicrous as a conductor flailing away with both hands, "beating time" with great effort while never once showing shape, phrasing, dynamics, etc. Reminding the choir of aspects carefully worked out in rehearsal and requiring their faithfulness is a conductor's job. Learning correct conducting patterns is important, but understanding the vital ingredients of the music is also important and essential. Many conducting classes would benefit from careful score study to enable knowledge of *what* to conduct, as a balance to *how* to gesture knowingly. Most conductors are intelligent enough to learn basic patterns, but are often dangerous because of lack of score knowledge. It is important to know both *how* to conduct and also *what* to conduct. There is a standard language or grammar of conducting which choral conductors notoriously and flagrantly violate. Often, a special set of signals, known only to those choir initiates, is employed which works by dent of repetition for that particular ensemble. Put that conductor in front of a new group or, heaven forbid, an instrumental ensemble, and he or she hasn't a prayer! Our striving should be to *look* like the music *sounds*, not like a caricature thereof. One more obser-

vation: a conductor cannot *make* anyone play or sing anything. Often, we get in the way of our groups by reaching toward them, hunching shoulders, grunting, groaning, stamping our feet, snapping our fingers, singing *with them* (that way, one can't *hear* them), and in general, expending much wasted energy which does not bring corresponding results. These are the conductors Ann Jones speaks about, who at the end of rehearsal are sweating and completely wasted physically, while their people ask: "What was *that* all about?" Almost without exception, *less* is *more* when conducting. In the same way that we expect recognizable English grammar when conductors *speak,* we expect appropriate conducting grammar when they *conduct.* Enough said!

Problem Areas: Notation

In *Creative Hymn Singing,* Alice Parker maintains that "notation is an aid to remembered sound." This is not license for taking liberties with what someone else has written, often called "decomposing," but for developing an awareness of the room and of the voices singing and instruments playing *in that room.* One may need to ask for shortened notes, lengthened notes, flute taken up the octave, baritones doubling basses at the upper octave, consonants placed well ahead of the beat, *poco staccato, poco legato,* etc. All of this can be overdone, to be sure, but usually one does not get *enough* change, dynamic flexibility, and attention to what is actually *sounding.* The musical "scribes and pharisees" among us balk at what they think is a violation of the printed page they hold so sacred, but the conductor's task is to allow the music to sound, being faithful to what is written, but not slavishly adhering to every "jot" and "tittle" in some misguided attempt to approach "correctness." Does this contradict earlier statements regarding "truth in the score"? I think not. Much subtlety in music simply cannot be notated. The essence of Gregorian chant, the anacrusic feeling of Baroque rhythms or their cross-bar phrasings, or the development over many measures of a Brahms vocal line—these are but a few examples of what notation *cannot* do. We should place responsibility on ourselves and the choir for doing what is in the total interest of the music, faithful to what is written, striving for the right sound in the room. Combining faithfulness to what is written with attention to singers' and players' capabilities, and always being aware of how it sounds, makes for lively performance.

Problem Areas: Dynamics

Requiring dynamic gradations on a wide scale is difficult, for it is easier to sing at a *mf* or a *f* level all the time with not much in between. Negotiating the complete range of the tonal spectrum, from very soft to very loud, is a difficult but worthy goal. Marking these dynamics can be very helpful along with placing responsibility on the singers or players to execute what is marked. Most choirs rarely plumb the outer edges of a dynamic spectrum, content to sit somewhere in the middle or to scream constantly. It need not be thus. Our study enables understanding, and with understanding comes blossoming of dynamic awareness. One qualification to the above regards young singers: teenage voices should not be pushed at either end of this spectrum. Too much soft singing, in my opinion, is as vocally unproductive as too much loud singing. Those teenage bodies, often slumped over in our rehearsals, need to be stimulated to energize sound but not to under or over sing. The wise director chooses carefully, listens well and continues to advocate the very best vocal principles in an attempt to allow younger voices to mature easily and gradually.

Problem Areas: Making Creative Choices within an Anthem

As a postscript to the earlier discussion of form and change in music, one should always be alert to possibilities in the music which are not written down. In a two part anthem, for instance, Jane Marshall has taught us that the sound of male voices on the upper line and female voices on the lower line is a fresh, unused sound. Usually, we simply place the female voices on the top part and the male voices on the other part without creatively looking at another possibility. Our study should intrigue us with alternate placing or voicing: another choir or choirs might be used, or a quartet or soloist from a separate location in the room might be effective. We should always look for ways to utilize balconies, aisles or a narthex area as alternatives to the choir loft. Anything antiphonal is an obvious choice. Naturally, the printed copy will not say: "another choir or soloist could sing from a balcony or in the aisles," or "a single soloist would be most effective." We must see these possibilities ourselves, still faithful to what is written. Singers can be scrambled in arrangement instead of seated sectionally, and can sing from balcony or aisle or even be seated *in* the congregation. Our ears and eyes open up possibilities for the sounds in the room.

Problem Areas: The Youth Musical

In the initial writing of this epistle in 1980, I tried to be constructive and not too critical of the youth "musical" movement. Everyone reading this will know what type of work I mean and will have a definite idea of what he or she likes or dislikes, or what he or she would program for an individual youth choir in church. I do not see my stance in this revision as taking to task those who do a steady diet of youth "musicals," nor to comfort those who never do them. I was fortunate in both Norman and Dallas to have groups capable of presenting a full tour program of anthems, handbells, etc., using some new literature especially prepared for the tour but relying on literature sung in the context of regular worship responsibility all year. I have toured with a "musical" like *Creation, A Reason to Rejoice* or *A Season to Celebrate,* and there are a few new compositions that give me hope for a future in this genre but, in general, our tour programs were based on yearly literature of the styles discussed earlier. I have seen very successful productions with lots of attention to lighting, costumes and drama, though that has never been my interest. I have seen touring groups who combined a mission work with a singing tour and, though I have not done this, I applaud those who have. In short, I believe that situations are so different that prescribing antidotes for specific problems is not helpful. One problem remains, however: some of my colleagues get trapped into such a steady diet of "musicals" that they run out of something with which to sustain their choirs each year. This becomes almost impossible as the worthy literature runs out.

One solution to this trap is to use literature sung during the year to design a "musical" with narration, dance, etc., which ties the individual anthems together. Many people have done this with great success. One obvious framework is utilization of a theme: "the church year," "suffering servant," "psalms, hymns and spiritual songs," etc. Thus, the good work done all year on anthems becomes the backbone of a touring program. One may then add as much lighting, costuming, drama, etc., as necessary or desired for the finished product. This is certainly a more difficult procedure than buying a ready-to-sing work, but has a good stewardship advantage in using what you have already done and is an excellent chance to promote creativity as the youth help plan and work out the details.

I will say again that I believe youth will respond to a balanced diet of anthems because they like variety and can recognize craftsmanship, especially with careful, patient leadership. We misjudge them, I believe, when we expect too little or when we attempt to snare their interest with second-rate musical and theological experiences. Once, after a workshop, a participant walked up and remarked: "It's easy for you to encourage these anthems by Schütz, Handel, Bach, and Haydn—you are in a big church in a big city with many advantages—you are a full-time director with study time available and you have opportunity to search out and study the best literature available. *My* young people, however, do not like Handel or Haydn and will not come if I do that type of music." My response closes this chapter and I do not intend it unkindly. The comment, "*My* young people do not like Brahms and Haydn and won't come if I choose this literature" was met with this response: "My experience is that 'they' *will* come and *will* like this varied diet I espouse if one chooses well, studies well and does not give up on them." Pogo was right: "We have found the enemy, and it is us."

6 CHANGING VOICES

Perhaps one of the most frustrating aspects of church youth choir work concerns junior high boys whose voices are changing. If boys are with girls in a junior high age choir, it is possible to separate them during part of the rehearsal with benefit to both. Most youth choirs, however, group junior high and senior high age singers together and one is immediately faced with the problem of voice classification for these changing boys and choice of repertoire to suit both *their* needs *and* those of the entire group. In other words, *where* do they sing, and *what* do they sing?

In a seventh through twelfth grade church choir, there may be some junior high age boys whose voices are already changed. They will probably be comfortable singing tenor or baritone-bass. Some boys never experience drastic change and gradually move from alto to tenor to baritone or bass. The problem or challenge is in keeping the interest of those boys who *do* experience vocal changes which leave them floundering and "squeaking" on a harmony part.

A junior high boy, accustomed to singing the melody in an "unchanged" voice, has to be guided and encouraged as change or mutation occurs. If a boy is unsure which notes will come out, how they will sound (with that ever-present "squeak") and, in addition, is asked to sing harmony—not melody—the chance of his loss from the group is great unless steps are taken to keep his interest active and his vocal development constant. Unless a director understands the process of change, acquires the skill of quickly assessing where to place these voices, works diligently on vocal foundation, and develops a knowledge of appropriate literature, boys will continue to be lost from church choral programs and perhaps from a lifetime of singing. It need not be so.

What about junior high girls in this same choral grouping? Though they do experience vocal change, it usually is not as dramatic as that of the boys. Classifying the girls should be based on strength and maturity of sound in both upper and lower range, vocal tessitura (where most of the notes lie) and voice quality. In my experience, very few junior high girls are true altos, nor are they high first sopranos. Most fit into the general range and quality category of second soprano. For seating after classification, I recommend dividing the junior high girls into two groups: Group I

53

sings soprano on a particular anthem while Group II sings alto. On the next anthem the groups switch, with Group I now singing alto and Group II soprano. This is not as convenient when there are both junior high and senior high girls and may involve movement or careful, creative seating. It *is* much better for their vocal development. In a time when so much popular music is sung in a lower register (heavy mechanism) with a "belting" quality, it is imperative that young female singers learn to use all of their available range. If we directors insist on vocalization throughout the range, no girl develops what I term the "alto-mentality: God did not intend for me to sing any note above fourth line 'd' in the treble clef." Similarly, no girl develops what I term the "soprano-mentality: Woe is me if I don't always sing the melody."

A further complication is voice classification by another director in a school or community choir. "Mrs. Smith has me singing alto in the St. Cecilia Girls Chorus," is the usual line. Sometimes I find the needs of the group have been placed ahead of what is best for individual vocal growth. "Good readers" are placed on alto without much regard for strength, maturity of sound or voice quality. This is vocal typecasting and works against what is espoused above. Yes, that upper register sound *is* breathy and the lower register (speaking voice range) carries better and *seems* fuller, but those young female singers lose in the long run unless encouraged to exercise their full range capability lightly with good vowel sounds and proper breath support.

Understanding the Process of Vocal Change (Mutation)

It is beyond the scope of this chapter to fully present materials discussed elsewhere. I strongly recommend, however, the reading of three articles by Dr. John M. Cooksey in the October, November and December 1977 issues of the *Choral Journal*. The title sounds foreboding but the information is presented clearly: "The Development of a Contemporary, Eclectic Theory for the Training and Cultivation of the Junior High School Male Changing Voice." Dr. Cooksey does a masterful job of presenting and summarizing three distinctive theories which emerged in the 1950s and 1960s about the junior high school male changing voice: those of Irvin Cooper, Frederick Swanson, and Duncan McKenzie.

To quote from the article:

> Irvin Cooper . . . proposed the cambiata plan. Dr. Frederick Swanson . . . conducted a major research project . . . discovering the 'adolescent bass.' Duncan McKenzie . . . continued

to espouse a 'middle-of-the-road' alto-tenor approach. Each proponent was persuasive and articulate, and each produced convincing empirical evidence supporting his own views.[6]

After presenting the views of each of the three and their numerous differences, Cooksey finds some points of agreement:

1. The voice change occurs at the onset of puberty, and is directly related to the development of primary and secondary sexual characteristics.
2. Most currently published literature is inadequate to fit the range and tessitura of the male changing voice.
3. Irregular growth rates in the vocal mechanism can make the voice unpredictable and difficult to control, particularly if it is forced into the wrong pitch range.
4. In groups of boys between the ages of twelve and fifteen, one might expect to find voices in many different stages of growth.
5. The rate in which voice changes occur varies with individuals.
6. Individual and group voice testing is necessary.
7. Teachers should help students to understand their voices during the change.
8. It is very important to establish good singing habits during this time.[7]

The ideas offered by the Cooksey articles form a basic framework of integrated concepts which focus upon range, tessitura, register delineation, and voice quality as primary factors in voice development.

To put it another way:

Because of the many challenges involved . . . such as the wide variability of range, tessitura, register delineation, and vocal agility among individuals . . . the task of dealing with these adolescent voices in the choral situation becomes highly complex, and at times, extremely difficult.[8]

For those of us in church situations with non-auditioned groups meeting weekly, a better understanding of changing voices and what to do with them can make a marked difference in choir performance and in individual enhancement of each boy's potential. If this is new territory, be brave. Our tendency is to blame the situation or fault the young people. You cannot hurt your boys by doing background reading, asking questions, seeking out a local junior high school director whose group sounds good, and adding to your knowledge. You *can* hurt them by ignorance of this very basic and natural series of changes and by treating them as if they

d in a more regular SATB situation. Cooksey summarizes
al situation:

As understanding and insight are achieved, the entire singing
experience for the junior high male becomes positive, healthy,
and exciting! As a result, the young man becomes more encouraged to continue his participation in choral activities later
on in life. He is not 'turned off' to being a part of the school
(or church) choir, and he seeks aggressively to expand his
musical experiences in many areas. This writer believes that
realistic and practical approaches to training and dealing with
the changing voice *can* be accomplished in the choral situation.[9]

Group Voice Testing Procedures

What is needed is a quick, painless way of assessing where voices
need to be singing. This is essential before literature can be chosen.
Though there are certain similarities, let me present a "Yarrington
Plan" for testing and seating, followed by a "Cooksey Plan" for
the same. The intent of both is a balance of speed and accuracy
in vocal designation.

Yarrington Plan

Boys
1. Girls sit in back, boys in front for initial test.
2. Tell the boys you are going to listen for *baritones* only. Ask
   them to sing *Jingle Bells* in the key of D major. (Starting note:
   f♯)
3. As they sing, some of the boys will obviously be in the lower
   octave. Tap them on the shoulder—these are your *baritones.*
4. Ask the rest of the boys to sing *Jingle Bells* again, this time
   in the key of A♭ major (starting note: third space c, treble
   clef). Tap on the shoulder those boys singing in the upper
   octave. These are your *unchanged* boys. Don't worry about
   the "wanderers" for the moment.
5. By a simple process, we have identified baritones and unchanged voices—those voices remaining are in some phase
   of change. There may be some boy altos in this group and
   there also may be some unchanged boys who did not really
   sing in their true, unchanged voice. As choir work begins,
   these boys usually relax and begin singing where it is most
   comfortable. One constantly audits each boy's vocal development and moves him into the proper classification.

56

Girls

1. Ask the girls to sing *Jingle Bells* in D major; listen for the strongest voices who are also singing effortlessly. Tap those on the shoulder, they sit.
2. Ask the remaining girls to sing *Jingle Bells* in A♭ major, listening to the strongest voices who are not forcing the sound.
3. Divide some who are seated with some of those standing into Group I. The rest become Group II.
4. Ideally, Group I will sing soprano on a particular anthem while Group II sings alto, then reverse on the next piece. With a seventh-twelfth grade group there will be some older girls who really should be singing either soprano or alto, and these can be accommodated with careful seating arrangements. *All* the female singers, whether soprano or alto, should be vocalized over a full range and encouraged to use all available notes with plenty of breath support and never too much vocal weight.

Seating

Here is a possible seating plan based on the above:

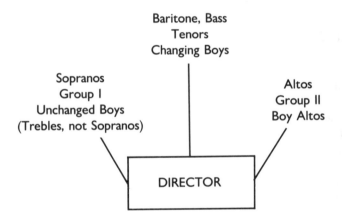

This arrangement allows auditing of the boys at all times, moving among them *while* they are singing, helping them with their part, and assessing their need to move into the next classification. An accompanist for rehearsal is not a luxury but a necessity.

General Vocal Ranges and Tessitura

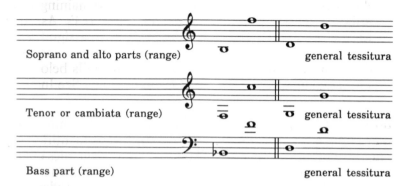

Soprano and alto parts (range)   general tessitura

Tenor or cambiata (range)   general tessitura

Bass part (range)   general tessitura

Group Voice Testing: Cooksey Plan

The following is a group testing procedure recommended by Dr. Cooksey:

1. Ask everyone to sing *America* in the key of C (B♭ will also work, particularly if there are a number of physically "more mature" boys in the choir).
2. Ask the boys to sing alone, in C. Listen for voices singing in the octave below middle C. As you walk around, point to the individuals in the section who are singing in the lower octave and tell them to remember this designation. These are your *baritones*.

   Those identified as baritones sing alone as a group. Check for any errors you have made. In cases where boys are not matching pitch, listen for notes sounding below correct pitches. If you have chosen voices which have not yet reached the baritone stage, you will hear their sound above the actual correct pitches being sung by the majority.
3. Ask the remaining boys (after the baritones are seated together as a section) to sing *America* in F or G (above middle C). Walk through the section and point to those who are obviously singing in the upper octave with ease. Also note the lightness of the vocal quality. These should be *Midvoice I's* and *Unchanged Voices*. These singers should be assigned to alto (SATB mixed chorus situation) or possibly *tenor*. As you listen to these voices, again, watch for boys singing in the falsetto register; some of these may be baritones or *Midvoice II's*.

4. For confirmation, unchanged male voices/Midvoice I's sing *America* in F or G (above middle C). The remaining voices to be auditioned should be *Midvoice II's* or *IIA's*. Ask them to sing *America* in B♭ (below middle C): then assign them to the tenor part. (The limitations of this part in most adult SATB music should be noted; if the range falls below E or F—below middle C—the part will be too low.) See Index for Voice Classification, p. 62.

Boys are very self-conscious in the seventh and eighth grades, and in a "mixed choir" situation do not want to be identified with the high-soprano part. In a male choir, the group dynamics change, and there is more flexibility in assigning these voices to higher parts. The following diagram shows one way to seat students in a mixed arrangement:

Soprano	Baritone	IIA's	Midvoice II	*	Alto

*Unchanged / Midvoice I

For Girls

Ask them to sing *America* in C or B♭. Point to the strongest voices who are also singing the notes with relative ease.

Also, ask everyone to sing *America* in f or g (above middle C), again pointing to the strongest voices who are not forcing the sound. Voices that have been identified in both segments may be divided evenly between soprano and alto. Listen for balance and uniformity of sound between the two groups. Voices that sing with more ease in the upper or lower keys should be assigned accordingly.

The remainder of the girls, with weaker voices, should be assigned fairly evenly between soprano and alto. The primary criteria for part classification are:

1. strength/maturity of sound in both upper and lower parts of range
2. vocal tessitura

3. voice quality (NOTE: girls' voices are also maturing at this
   age and have not settled into a real alto sound)[10]
Recommended earlier in the chapter were three articles by Dr.
John Cooksey in the 1977 *Choral Journal.* This material presents
in more depth the nature and scope of work with boys' changing
voices.
Here is an example from these articles:

> In my own teaching experience with junior high boys, I have
> found that voice mutation occurs most dramatically in the
> eighth grade for the majority, and usually tapers off consid-
> erably by the middle of the ninth grade year. It is tricky business
> to detect the beginning of the change since the vocal cords
> and larynx do not grow overnight. Instead, the voice changes
> take place gradually at first (usually in the seventh grade, ages
> twelve to thirteen), then *accelerate* during a three to twelve
> month period on the average (from ages thirteen to fourteen).
> It is during this time of accelerated growth (not just with the
> voice, but also with other physiological phenomena) that the
> voice changes become *most noticeable.*
>
> I suppose these changes *are* dramatic and rapid if considered
> as one part of the overall development growth of the individual.
> Too often, however, the early signs associated with the begin-
> ning stages of voice mutation are not recognized (such as the
> loss of higher notes, increased breathiness in the sound, etc.)
> and full attention is given only to the crux period of mutation.
> Granted, in some cases, dramatic voice changes do take place,
> and within a very short length of time. It is certainly true that
> some boys go through the change much more rapidly than
> others and that for each grade and year one *will* find voices
> in all stages of development. Individual variations on the theme
> are the rule, not the exception, in junior high school. These
> variations, however, *do* conform to a stable sequence or pattern
> of events. Thus voice mutation does occur in identifiable
> development stages. It is the *rate of change* and the entry/
> exit points of pubertal voice development which are so
> variable.[11]

Building a Solid Vocal Foundation

As stated earlier, most church youth choirs have a combination
of junior /senior high voices so that voice "building" for everyone,
including the changing junior high male, must be done in the
context of rehearsal together. After the initial classification, as
rehearsals proceed, the seating recommended (which places boys

in the front) allows the director to audit the way they sound *and* look. If possible, schedule some sessions early in the year just with the changing voice boys. Call these sessions "fourth-quarter" classes and encourage the following:

1. *Principles of Good Posture and Breath Support*
   A good way to begin is by raising the arms over the head, then bringing them down slowly, leaving the *rib cage* high and relaxing the shoulders. Ask the boys to find their *rib cage* (not their chest) with either hand. Encourage them to stand tall, then rotate the head slowly from side to side and in a clockwise or counterclockwise manner. They should also be able to rotate their shoulders forward or backward. Remind them that learning the correct stance for golf, tennis, diving, batting, etc., takes time . . . *and practice.* It doesn't feel "natural" at the beginning.

   Cooksey recommends inhaling audibly, "sucking air in through puckered lips. (This controls the rate of air flow going to the lungs and permits the chest and abdominal areas to expand gradually.) Inhale slowly and evenly. At the end of inhalation, immediately expel the air by hissing, *'ssss.' "* [12]

   Further, he directs: "suck the air in, hiss *'sss'*. . . then connect with a voice (sung) sound, *'sah.'* The *'sah'* should be a comfortable note for all voices. (Mixed choir: middle C, octave below for baritones. Individual voices, use F [above middle C] for boy sopranos and *Midvoice I's*; middle C for *Midvoice II's*; F [below middle C] for baritones.)" [13]

   He further refines this process by asking singers to whisper *"ah"* upon inhalation, then whisper *"hah"* upon exhalation. Phonation occurs on *"hah".* Then a natural breath is taken, as the final step in this sequence. [14]

2. *Key problems related to posture and breath support are enumerated by Dr. Cooksey:*
   a. Failure to hold chest up and to relax the abdominal area during inhalation. (I much prefer asking them to hold up the *rib cage,* because it helps eliminate raising the shoulders.)
   b. Shallow breathing: too much chest action, raising shoulders.

61

Index for Voice Classification in Junior High School Male Adolescents

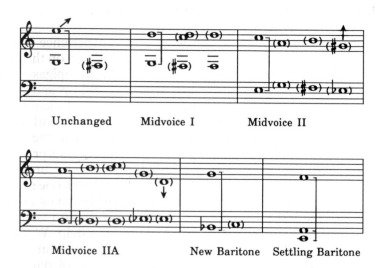

Unchanged   Midvoice I   Midvoice II

Midvoice IIA   New Baritone   Settling Baritone

*Bracketed notes—primary range boundaries
Notes in parentheses—case exceptions[16]

Mean Ranges and Tessituras for the Voice Change Stages

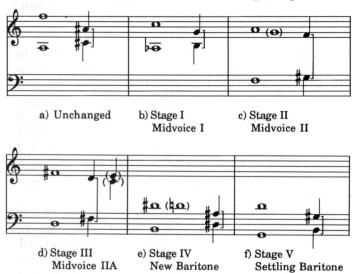

a) Unchanged   b) Stage I   c) Stage II
                  Midvoice I   Midvoice II

d) Stage III   e) Stage IV   f) Stage V
   Midvoice IIA   New Baritone   Settling Baritone

*Bracketed notes—tessituras[17]

c. Reverse muscular action . . . that is, the stomach pulls inward as the student breathes.

d. Consciously pushing the stomach in or out.[15]

3. *Solutions to some of the key problems*

a. In general, the easiest way for a boy to experience what is going on in the breathing process is to lie down on the floor, placing a hand on the stomach area (really, the epigastrium). Easy, relaxed breathing will move that hand up and down. A book or the director's hand over that of the student is also helpful. Standing with shoulders against a wall with director's fist in the same area allows the student to "feel" the flow of breath. Most of the time, students are surprised by the entire action and realize they have not been breathing in this manner. Sometimes they can pair off with one student checking the breathing of the other, placing hands at each side of the body to check expansion. This can result in a certain amount of silliness, but humor can help. When we are self-conscious we react to cover our discomfort in various ways, such as laughing. Don't let it get out of hand, but realize the dynamics of the situation.

b. Get some of your leaders up in front to demonstrate for everyone else.

c. Have patience and don't spend an inordinate amount of time on this aspect.

4. *Coordination of breath and sound*

a. It is important to get across the concept that once breath is taken (inhaled) it should result in a sound. There cannot be a "stop" between inhalation and actual phonation. The concept is that of a circle and the attack is not abrupt, jolted, struck, or forced. It *is,* as the saying goes, "on the breath."

b. Cooksey recommends use of the "hiss" connected to *"ah"* or *"oh"* on a simple scale passage of 1 2 3 4 3 2 1. He suggests the same idea using a "buzzing *vvvv"* or a *"K."* For more specific examples, I refer the reader to the three articles in the *Choral Journal.*

Between the principles espoused in the chapters on "Establishing a Sound," "Changing Voices," and "Private and Class Voice Instruction," the reader should be able to feel more comfortable about voice building, explaining the process *simply* and tailoring vocalises that really accomplish the purpose of better, more relaxed, well-produced sound. Too much explanation will not bring results. Too little knowledge will never move the group forward. As much individual instruction as possible—either privately, in a class setting, or in sectional rehearsals—will pay big dividends.

Appropriate Literature

To quote Irvin Cooper:
> May I suggest that ninety percent of all published adult choral music is completely out of the range of junior high boys? Grade of difficulty is not the issue; it is strictly a matter of range. However much you like a certain composition and wish to use it, if the vocal ranges or general tessitura do not agree with what you have, it just cannot be sung successfully by a junior high mixed group, unless of course you have a small, hand-picked group of exceptional voices from grade nine only.[18]

The good news is that you are aware of what is going on with your changing voices, and have quickly and simply classified everyone. You have also worked diligently on building a solid vocal foundation and "they" really do sound good. The bad news is that choosing the music for the group is one of your most difficult assignments. Generally speaking, here are some principles to guide you:

1. Unison music rarely works for everyone because it forces the changing voices into higher and/or lower notes than they can easily produce. All those folk anthems which sound so nice with changed voices won't work "un-tailored" for the entire group.

2. At the risk of oversimplification, let me suggest a procedure for an anthem which *does* work. The anthem used as an example is:

   Everywhere I Go by Natalie Sleeth (Choristers Guild CGA-171). After carefully looking at range and tessitura:
   a. Phrase 1 ("Everywhere I go") is sung by *girls only.*
   b. Phrase 2 ("If I call upon him") is sung by *boys only.*
   c. Phrase 3 ("Never will I fear") *sung by everyone* (lowest two notes may be too low).
   d. Middle section ("He is with me . . . He will be") *boys only.* ("From his path") *girls only.*
   e. Final two part section: The upper vocal line may be divided as at the beginning (phrase 1, phrase 2, phrase 3). The lower vocal line may be divided between girls and boys in the same manner.

This will make no sense unless you study the anthem. The principle is simple, however: individual anthems must be studied to see where the notes lie. Taking notes up the octave, leaving out certain notes, tailoring the part for the changing voices is the only way to work. Many publishers have anthems specifically written with these voices in mind, including Cambiata Press. Again, each anthem must be scrutinized to see if it fits the singers you have. Dr. Cooksey makes several suggestions:

1. Be ready for some compromises. Most music is not written to suit changing voices. If each individual knows his limitations, some music can be selected which has some notes which test the lower and upper limits of the singing range. Use common sense in urging students not to force or push for the few notes they may not have.

2. Be ready to arrange and add accompanying lines to unison melodies. Remember, students will not sing melodies or parts which are not suitable for their voice change stage.

3. Each vocal part should be examined to make sure that extreme demands are not placed on the voice. Selections which demand great tone control for the long phrase should be avoided, as well as those which have melismas calling for rapid adjustments at the laryngeal level.

4. Choose music to suit the breath control capabilities of young adolescent boys. Young boys have a tendency to expend too much air too soon. Long phrases in the upper range, for example, will cause undue strain and tension if proper breath support is not developed.

5. Be sure that in three part music the tessitura for the lower part is *not too high* for the baritones.

6. Most SSA and SAB music is unsuitable for the junior high changing voice.

7. Avoid trite texts and many "pop" tunes.

8. Some vocal arrangements should "spotlight" the changing voice section or new/settling baritones. If they are given the melody, for example, during a section of the piece, this does wonders for their confidence level.

9. Music which has obvious rhythmic, melodic, harmonic interest is very satisfying to students of this age. (This excludes much of the "trite" pop tunes which are being published today.)

10. Give students a variety of literature.[19] (See the chapter on "Choosing the Music.")

Coda

Finally, be patient. It takes time to become comfortable with this important area of choir work. Work with changing voices *and* temperaments is a mission field all its own. One cannot work exclusively with changing voices in a situation encompassing *all* voices in a junior high/senior high mixed choral situation, but the knowledge of the process is essential to the development of the *entire* group. That you care about them, that you recognize that this is a changing time for *all of them,* as bodies are growing and developing, will be evident in your awareness, sympathy, and concern. You may not be successful every time, and there will be those occasions when all will seem lost, but your skillful handling of the situation will enable their increased confidence. These changing voices and personalities are certainly worth that effort.

Endnotes

[6] Cooksey, John M. "The Development of a Contemporary, Eclectic Theory for the Training and Cultivation of the Junior High School Male Changing Voice," *Choral Journal* Part I, October, 1977, Part II, November, 1977, Part III, December 1977. Page 5, October 1977.
[7] Cooksey, John M. Part I, October 1977, page 13.
[8] Cooksey, John M. Part III, December 1977, page 5.
[9] Cooksey, John M. Part III, December 1977, page 5.
[10] Cooksey, John M. From unpublished workshop notes.
[11] Cooksey, John M. Part II, November 1977, page 12.
[12] Cooksey, John M. Part III, December 1977, page 11.
[13] Cooksey, John M. Part III, December 1977, page 11.
[14] Cooksey, John M. Part III, December 1977, page 11.
[15] Cooksey, John M. Part III, December 1977, page 11.
[16] Cooksey, John M. From unpublished workshop notes.
[17] Cooksey, John M. From unpublished workshop notes.
[18] Cooper, Irvin, "Changing Voices in Junior High," Carl Fischer. page 12.
[19] Cooksey, John M. From unpublished workshop notes.

7 PRIVATE AND CLASS VOICE INSTRUCTION

If vocal training on the part of the director is adequate and if time permits, one may offer private or class voice sessions to the young people in the choir. Here good vocal habits stressed in rehearsal can be more closely monitored, one-on-one relationships established, and availability of soloists fostered. Lessons may be on a scholarship basis with a certain number of sessions given in exchange for extra service to the music program in the areas of telephoning, robe care, music filing, or assistance with one or more younger choirs. This involvement solves the question of payment and serves to develop leadership in vital areas of concern to the total program of music ministry. Sometimes those most talented do not participate because of limited time and, while this may prove disappointing, those who most need the vocal work are helped.

In addition to vocal aid, the sessions allow for friendly, informal counseling which at times alleviates behavioral problems apparent in rehearsal. Needs met in this way help the student, the group, and the director, and can be one of the most enjoyable aspects of your work. One gets to know these young singers in a special way and lifelong friendships can result. The fact that you care enough to spend time with them individually comes across stronger than any words, no matter how inspirational. They may share experiences, concerns, or problems with you and your willingness not to attempt solutions but simply to listen serves their need.

One needs to decide whether an individual would best prosper in a private setting, or with two or three others in a class session where an audience is provided and the efforts of the others supported. A class environment may take away fear of the process. Later, those who show special aptitude may move on to private study as they gain confidence. If a class session *is* adopted, all work on the basic vocal habits together, but each student is heard individually at every lesson. Let us consider what these basic vocal habits entail.

Breathing

With a voice class or with a private student, ask for good singing posture—elevated rib cage, shoulders relaxed. When breath is taken, horizontal expansion below the rib cage, at the sides, and across the back is experienced. This physical movement is outward and downward, not up and toward the collarbones. Combined with attention to a relaxed throat as one takes a cold air breath, these two steps work for increased vocal function. In private or class sessions the sequence would be:

1. Lie flat on your back, placing your hand below your rib cage and breathe easily: if the breath moves the body upward, raising the chest and shoulders, one hand may be placed on the chest with the instruction not to move either the chest or the shoulders. Gradually, students develop a feeling akin to blowing up a balloon and the breath causes the body to expand horizontally, not vertically. This is a *learned* response. Make sure that it is the breath causing expansion and not some physical action on the part of the student.
2. Move to a flat wall, placing your body against it, hands (thumbs forward) below the rib cage to feel the expansion.
3. Move away from the wall, placing both hands on your sides at the bottom of the rib cage and breathe, taking care not to raise unduly the upper part of the body. This is the how-you-hold-your-instrument aspect of the lesson. When working with a class, students may pair off; one breathes, the other checks the breathing to be sure the breath causes the desired horizontal expansion.

Vocal Attack

Step two in the process involves "hitching" the breath to the sound so that the voice begins on-the-breath and is not forced, struck, or startled into being. The "yawn-sigh" mentioned earlier and the five-note descending scale are two exercises to be used profitably here. In addition, hymns sung with a neutral syllable *pahm* or *hoh* staccato, or *loo* or *loh* legato, establish a feel for using the breath *in conjunction* with the sound. The initial attack is thus on-the-breath, but not *breathy*.

Resonance

Step three involves activating resonance or "ping" even though we know that the voice cannot be *placed* anywhere. We *do* feel sensations in the throat, cheekbones and head, and we add this valuable component to the work on breathing and vocal attack. Resonance, *not nasality*, is added. Here are other exercises to accomplish this goal:

1. Descending five-note scale on *NAH (NnnAH, NnnAH, NnnAH, NnnAH, NnnAH)* or *MAH*

2. Descending five-note scale on *NAH* or *MAH* slurring two notes together.
3. Descending five-note scale on *WINnn* or *WONnn* with emphasis on the *"N"* or *"M."*

The object of these simple exercises is to establish a "hummy" feeling before opening to the vowel. Encourage students to carry this resonant feeling over into the sound, establishing a "point" but not creating nasality. *"HUNG-OH"* or *"HUNG-AH"* is also effective. Ask for a tall *"OH"* or *"AH,"* closing the lips lightly and keeping tall vowel shape in back and resonant hum in front. This may also be sung on a descending five-note scale.

Range

Working on increased range involves attempting both higher and lower notes than seem comfortable to the student at first. The vocalises of fire sirens, whistles, etc., used with younger singers to establish "head voice" or "lighter mechanism" can work effectively with girls in a private or class session. Many of these singers have sung basically in only one register—a "chesty" or "lower-register" or "heavy-mechanism" sound. Developing an upper register is a must if range is to increase. For the boys, singing in falsetto helps achieve the feeling of upper register and facilitates the register "shift" from lower sound to upper sound. Many boys have never sung in falsetto. While it may come easily for some, for others it will take several sessions (with patience) to establish this sound. Unless some effort is made with boys to establish a type of upper-register sound, many boys will suffer from a very small range, and experience frustration, tension, and ugly, nonproductive sounds. This important area is treated more fully in vocal textbooks and I encourage their use. One point is important: nothing is "broken" at any time. Both boys and girls experience a "shift" when going from one register of the voice to another. One may describe this change in many ways but for most young people the "melding" of registers is crucial to their vocal progress. For both boys and girls, downward vocalizing in a medium range helps in this "melding" process. Using the first part of *Joy to the World,* for instance, starting lightly on top and letting the voice fill out as it descends, is useful. A simple downward scale obviously accomplishes the same purpose.

Everything thus mentioned is equally effective in private or class sessions when simplicity is the watchword. Those readers knowledgeable in vocal matters will recognize that I have attempted to state the case simply and to give simple exercises. Obviously, there is much to know and one's experience is invaluable. There are many means by which we attempt to foster good vocal function and I would hope that this chapter would serve as a beginning point to whet and stimulate appetite in this regard.

As in vocal warm-ups for the entire youth choir, complicated vocalises found in so many handbooks defeat the very purpose for which they are printed because of their difficulty. Simple exercises devised by the teacher and tailored for individual needs are always better. Anthems and hymns with limited range are excellent as a diet, and a unison or two part anthem or hymn, used in this way, makes wonderful material for an offertory, a church school class solo, or special music for a board meeting or fellowship dinner. Additional useful material may be found in collections of popular musicals such as *Finian's Rainbow, The Sound of Music, Fiddler on the Roof,* etc. Most ranges here are medium and I find youth eager to work on this material, most of which is well-crafted and worthy. We should examine all possible resources, not limiting ourselves to those items considered "sacred," as we strive to enable students to *sound* better.

If you are interested in working privately with some of your young people, I encourage active pursuit of books and periodicals, auditing of good private voice teachers and attendance at events sponsored by organizations such as NATS (National Association of Teachers of Singing). Bringing in a guest voice teacher for several sessions with your young people stimulates interest and furthers one's own knowledge. Perhaps the private-class voice approach is not possible because of lack of time or inexperience in vocal training. However, if attempted, it may be a valuable addition to the continuing work on good vocal habits with the entire choir. Again, there is no magic in helping a private student to sing properly and beautifully. The "basics" already mentioned have to be established. By patient, careful work, students can attain a kind of sound which makes possible stylistic performance of a wide variety of literature, and also opens opportunity for solo and ensemble work. The establishment of a climate where personal relationships on a one-to-one basis develop is an added benefit.

8 PLEASURES AND PROBLEMS OF THE TOUR

I am one who believes in the old-fashioned puritanical ethic of doing what you are supposed to do, being responsible to others, and carrying through on what you begin. This brands me as a "kook" at the outset. I believe that young people can and will give responsible service over the long term, will get their weary bodies and even more weary throats (the hoarseness moves right along from football, to basketball, to swimming, etc.: it is *never over*) to your local establishment of worship and croak something out . . . even at 8:30 a.m. They never sound quite like they did at Sunday or Wednesday evening rehearsal (a gross understatement) but they *are* there and they *do* serve.

Choir directors, like scout leaders, den mothers, and others who work with volunteers know, however, that responsible service in itself is usually not sufficient motivation. Most of us need a tangible reward of some kind, whether a badge, a certificate, an award or a trip. In a day and time when young people are pulled so many ways, a trip or exchange with another youth choir can be a healthy way of keeping their interest and giving the entire group a worthy goal.

Lyle Schaller suggests that trips or tours can be very positive, unifying experiences as the group shares in:
1. Planning for the trip
2. Taking the trip
3. The return and reminiscences complete with pictures.[20]

Background

In Norman, Oklahoma, tours with the McFarlin youth and handbell choirs were initiated only after regular worship leadership resulted in a choir whose musical achievements matched its responsible service. A trip provided a wider audience for the group, giving incentive which encouraged active participation in choir activities. Our primary purpose (serving our local congregation) was balanced by a long-range goal which kept excitement and anticipation high all year. Significant leadership benefits developed as the young people planned a route, raised money, and set up attendance requirements. Other churches were inspired to begin

71

or revitalize their own groups because of the success of these tour concerts. Over a period of many years, I observed that youth will give themselves to a long-term commitment of this type, balanced by regular weekly worship leadership. Confidence in leadership resources within the group can be fostered as a valuable by-product.

In Norman, the tour grew from a three-day, two-state excursion to trips of longer duration, including two national tours. In Dallas, I inherited the tradition of an annual tour and found that many of the same principles articulated above applied there as well. Perhaps these principles served even better in Dallas, where, as stated earlier, the young people found themselves together in this group only *one* hour a week. A trip provided a means of unifying the group dynamic. I believe that attendance requirements must be set and enforced by the youth and their council. I believe that each person must covenant with the group to represent the church well (there goes my old-fashioned streak again) and interact effectively with everyone else on the trip.

I found it helpful to question the process and procedures repeatedly. Sometimes commitment was higher, numbers better or quality more solid, but I felt this a venture worthy of the time and energy necessary for its fulfillment. In Norman, as in Dallas, a tour provided incentive for youth to feel part of a successful group, helped the congregation sense their mission in support of such a group, and provided a plateau of arrival for those coming up from the younger choirs. Never again will these young people be at precisely this same stage in their lives and never again will possibilities exist for such a trip. We toured honestly and with good conviction, using procedures outlined below.

The Route

A primary location was selected or an invitation accepted, and planning commenced to get the choir there and back again. Personal contact is always the best way to set up a concert stop and much preferable to the following conversation (simulated) with a total stranger: "Hello, this is John Yarrington. Wouldn't you like to publicize, feed and house my group of 50 teenagers from Saint Swithens in the Swamp Youth Choir?" The usual response is similar to that given to the myriad of long-distance callers hawking magazines, special services, or products. It is increasingly difficult to "get out a crowd" for one's own services, not to mention for a touring choir, no matter how fine. This fact, coupled with the knowledge that many, many groups are out touring every year, makes a host wary of accepting your "wonderful opportunity." Personal contact by a member of your congregation with someone in a host congregation can produce results, as can a reciprocal arrangement in which you return the favor of hosting at a later date.

However the route is selected, one must know destinations and timetables before money can be raised. We have found that an attempt to cover more than 250 or 300 miles a day results in weary singers and frazzled sponsors. Though it may seem too obvious to mention, some trips will involve time changes, which must also be considered when planning. If you gain time, you may be fortunate. If you lose time, however, you could be in deep trouble. Jumping off the bus, setting up, gulping down a meal, and singing a concert in a frantic state is not considered good form and seldom works.

Once the route is known, the cost of the trip can be calculated and a monetary goal set. A major expenditure is that of the chartered bus or buses (which provide needed equipment space, air conditioning, and an experienced driver). Though expensive, I have always felt this a necessary component of the trip.

Often we planned a mid-tour break which involved hotel lodging and one catered meal. The hotel and meal expenses were financed through group fund-raising plus an individual assessment ($25-50). Scholarships were available for those who needed assistance.

In Norman, we spent most of our year in fund-raising activities with projects like bottle drives, car washes, paper drives, talent shows, greenery sales, church dinners, refreshment booths for local sporting events, and offerings on the road. You can certainly add to this list.

In Dallas, the fund-raising tradition was that of a dinner theatre with a bazaar, followed by a seated dinner (served by the youth) and a variety show (starring the same youth). After dinner and the show, an auction of ten or fifteen donated items was held. My predecessor, Boo Owens, used this plan for a number of years with great success. Parents together with young people headed up all the committees (food, decorations, costumes, bake sale, auction, etc.). As much as possible, items such as meat, paper goods, etc., were donated so that overhead was low. Tickets were required for the dinner, show and bazaar.

Each year, a general theme gave focus to decorations, costumes, and music. One theme, *Come, Take a Ride on the Love Boat,* featured a bazaar with shipboard activities such as movies, shuffleboard, etc., and suggested many ideas for decorations including large travel posters. Minimal costuming (white shirts, shorts, sailor hats, blue bow ties) for the choir was easily arranged and music related to the theme was plentiful.

For several years, the themes were taken from a publication by Hal Leonard with musical arrangements by Mark A. Brymer. *American Pop* was the title of one such collection or revue which featured 25 pop classics in unison/two part (Leonard 08637060) or SATB (Leonard 08637052). A production package included musical score and instrumental parts, accompaniment cassette, publicity posters, and programs. Another such revue, *S.R.O.* (Standing Room Only) was divided into four acts: "Those Vaudeville Days," "The Best of Broadway," "The Big Band Radio Hour," and "Songs of the Silver Screen"; unison/two part (Leonard 08639176), SATB (Leonard 08639172). Again, posters, accompaniment track, etc., are included and the arrangements are well crafted.

74

The "S.R.O." theme, for instance, featured a cabaret beforehand (one of the songs in the show) including a clown, face painting, a magic show, a cake walk and a silent auction. The dining room at the church was decorated in black and white, the choir outfitted in white shirts, black slacks, black vests, tissue paper carnations and black paper top hats. This was done easily and inexpensively.

Live accompaniment (piano/percussion) allowed for transposition for some soloists who needed lower or higher keys than printed. The advantage of these revues is that one can use them as blueprints for one's own individual group. Some songs may be deleted or others added. The variety of literature makes possible the involvement of a large number of young people in solos, duets, and speaking parts. One year, because of limited rehearsal time, I decided to try using the prerecorded track. Every youth was provided a cassette tape, and encouraged to listen and memorize. The voices on the tape were light and on pitch, providing a good vocal model for the young people. Soloists were cautioned that once the tape started, they would have to sing with it—no stops, no change of key! There were no major mistakes and the total effect was very professional.

This dinner theatre format had many advantages:

1. *One major fund-raiser.* It was not necessary to wash cars, collect bottles, or sell greenery, grapefruit, or light bulbs. (We usually cleared between $4,000.00 and $6,000.00 in this one event so no other fund-raising was needed.)
2. *Significant parent involvement.* The parents preferred this one-time effort over multiple activities because their garages and houses were stacked full of fruitcakes, magazines, boxes of candles, and cartons of light bulbs which they bought but did not really want or need!
3. *Strong congregational support.* Because we were not constantly asking the congregation to buy something from the youth, they were more than happy to participate in this event; support came from across the entire church, even from those who did not have youth in the choir.

In addition to the positive aspects outlined above, there were other benefits of a dinner theatre production:

1. *Memorization.* This type of show requires memorization for effectiveness. Singers discover that they *can* memorize, a skill which will be most useful throughout the year. The look and

sound of a youth choir, with music well memorized, is altogether different from the slouching stance (music held low, etc.) which many of us experience, particularly on Sunday mornings. With music memorized they even *watch* the director!

2. *Movement.* For most youth, moving or dancing to music comes very easily. Getting them to move in front of peers, family, and friends is another matter, but it *can* be done and is a valuable experience.

3. *Mastery.* Standing with presence before an audience as soloist or member of an ensemble builds self-esteem and personal confidence. Many are the young people who have blossomed after such an experience.

4. *Momentum.* Singing "lighter" literature is a welcome respite for director and chorus. Nothing is so constant as preparing music for worship Sunday after Sunday. A change of pace *once* a year is profitable for the group.

Housing

Pairing off in twos and staying in homes each evening is ideal, for it solves one of the main problems on the road—breakfast! Sleeping bags in churches is an alternative, but most churches are neither equipped with bathrooms to handle a large group nor with electrical circuits to handle the hair dryers of both the girls *and* boys! Fellowship with host families is fostered with home stays and your group then enjoys a morning reunion with their fellow choir members at each stop. It was at this morning time when our tour group had devotions and shared events of the past evening. This event set the tone for the day; announcements were made, then everyone boarded the bus for the next stop.

Publicity

The usual press release kit containing pictures, posters, and records or tapes helps local sponsors publicize the event of your coming. A visiting group takes a chance on an audience, particularly on an "off night" during the week. These publicity materials should go out well in advance. A wise host will try to schedule your group in conjunction with a church supper, a youth night or an area youth rally. No one wants to sing for three people and the on-duty janitor. This is an experience not recommended for inspiring the group to its highest potential. I *do* believe, however, that the possibility of small crowds should be discussed with the group. Their responsibility is to sing to the best of their ability regardless of how many people are present. My young people know the "Do your best no matter what" speech and, more than that, they know that I believe it!

Program Content

From previous statements it is apparent that I espouse a concert tour program embracing literature sung for worship throughout the year, supplemented by selections from a larger work, handbells, dance, dramatic readings, etc. It is useful to prepare more music than can be presented at any one concert so that interest remains high at each stop. Double and triple-casting of soloists is also another way to ensure high quality of effort in performance. If good instrumentalists are available within the group, they can be used to advantage both to accompany the choir and to play solo literature. Often on our tours, the women of the choir prepared one or more anthems as did the men, adding a bit more program variety. Costumes are up to individual choice and robes are perhaps easiest. In recent years we have worn dark slacks or skirts and brightly colored shirts, sometimes in the same color, other times with a rainbow effect. Some groups spend a great deal of money on outfitting everyone alike but I have not felt a major expenditure necessary.

Attendance Requirements

Early in the year, the choir council sets strict attendance requirements which include rehearsal and service responsibility, as well as participation in fund-raising activities. The usual pattern is to allow two or three unexcused absences. Responsibility is placed upon individual members to call their section leader or choir council member in advance to sign out *before* their absence. Sickness is always an excuse but needs to be monitored. There are the usual conflicts with school activities, jobs, and family schedules. Because of these everyone did not go on tour. When unusual circumstances arose, choir members were expected to appear before the choir council to plead their case. I always found the young people much stricter than I would have been about such matters. Those who had been faithful in attendance took a dim view of someone who conveniently was not there when the work was done, but wanted to go on the trip just the same. Once the choir members really believe that their council is going to administer the attendance requirements fairly and that the director will support their decisions, a sense of honesty prevails and the work of preparation is made much easier.

Covenant Card

Prior to the actual trip, we ask each member and parent to sign a card such as the one shown below. This card is one way of communicating your expectations of each choir member while on the trip. In addition you will also need a release form for the choir member to travel with you which complies with your state laws.

Choir Member	I covenant myself to the group, accepting responsibility not only for myself, but for other group members. I pledge to act responsibly, to think about consequences, and to do nothing which would in any way reflect badly on the fine tradition of the group, my obligation as a Christian young person, my home or parents, or my church.
Parent	I accept responsibility for this covenant between my child and the Choir. I understand that, if the covenant is violated, my child may have to leave the tour and I will be called upon to provide necessary transportation.
Youth	signature _____
Parent	signature _____

I cannot say that all conduct on every trip has been above reproach. Many of you will have your own stories to tell—some humorous, others not so. Some young people make poor choices, and even, in some cases, endanger themselves or someone else. Hosts sometimes allow activities or behavior not in keeping with tour rules. Each choir member must then act responsibly with his or her best judgment in that particular circumstance. I remember the youth who, when driving around town after a concert with a group of young people from the host church, asked to be taken home when beer was purchased at a local convenience store. This took real courage—the kind most difficult to muster. In most cases, choir members feel responsible to uphold their covenant. If something specific happens in violation of that covenant, the director and choir council consider each case individually. Your group looks to you for leadership. Young people are basically fair and they want their comrades treated fairly. They are also pretty justice-minded at this age and are quick to see discrepancies between talk and action. I remind each choir member that the trip is optional but *conduct* on the trip is not.

An additional benefit of the covenant card is permission for hospital care, signed by parent or guardian.

On the Road

Once the group departs the choir council is in charge of checking roll, stowing equipment, and helping to make enroute decisions as necessary. There are assigned duties, such as carrying risers, checking music, loading and unloading luggage, taking responsibility for stands and props, and bus cleanup.

We provide a printed note of thanks to be signed by the youth and left with the host family. We also encourage our young people to send a personal note *after* they return home.

Coda

Touring is satisfying and rewarding and, with careful planning, can be a positive experience. Singing together each night builds musical rapport and community is fostered. If approached honestly and with conviction, touring can be a worthwhile endeavor.

In review, the following are steps to development and nurturing of a successful youth choir.

Getting Started

Planning a specific event will attract, and offering regular responsibility for worship leadership will sustain.

Establishing a Sound

Patient and consistent nurturing is essential in the development of tone, vowel beauty, text intelligibility, and style consciousness.

Studying and Conducting

There is no substitute for careful, wise and appropriate choice in literature. Careful *choice* entails taking into account available personnel—not what we wish we had, but what we have! There is no substitute for intensive *study of* these choices, opening up possibilities for creative teaching.

Private and Class Voice Lessons
Additional opportunities for individual vocal nurture may be offered to supplement work done in rehearsal.

Changing Voices
Understanding and working effectively with changing voices is a first priority for success in youth choir work.

This is a unique time in the lives of young persons who have a freshness of approach and an openness to new experiences, thoughts, and ideas. There is something about working with youth choirs in church that defies description. The energy channeled into creative music-making, the rewards of leadership development, the establishment of special friendships, and the fostering of community are richly satisfying to both youth and directors.

In poetic fashion, Eric Johnson expresses these feelings of love and joy in *The Love of God:*

The love of God flows deep and strong, like a river that slowly runs to the sea and carries us evermore in the flow that will last eternally. The love of God flows soft and sure, refreshing our days like an evening breeze and carries us evermore in the flow that will last eternally. As the years come and go, as our lives spread and grow, there is something we can trust to always be so. When we're feeling despair, when we feel no one cares, it's a comfort to know God will always be there. The love of God flows through our lives with the solace and joy that God's spirit sends, and carries us evermore in the flow without end. The love of God flows like the dove, with its wings spread toward heaven, alive and free, and carries us evermore in the flow that will last eternally. God's love is deep and strong, God's love is soft and sure; God's love flows through our lives.

[20] Schaller, Lyle "The Pendulum Swings" in Choristers Guild *Letters*. May, 1982, pp. 161-164.

ABOUT THE AUTHOR

John Yarrington has successfully demonstrated the methods, techniques and philosophy of youth choir work through his service at the McFarlin Memorial United Methodist Church in Norman, Oklahoma and at the First United Methodist Church in Dallas, Texas. In both churches, his work with youth choirs was outstanding and served as a model for others around the country. In August of 1989 he began his present position as Director of Music and Arts at Pulaski Heights United Methodist Church in Little Rock, Arkansas.

After graduating from the University of Oklahoma with a Bachelor of Music Education Degree, Yarrington completed the Master of Sacred Music Degree at the Union Theological Seminary in New York, where he studied with Sergius Kagen, Madeleine Marshall, Abraham Kaplan, and William Gephart. Graduate studies at the University of Oklahoma under Dr. B.R. Henson and Dr. Dennis Shrock led to completion of the Doctor of Musical Arts Degree from that institution.

He is an active contributor to the work of the Choristers Guild, and his writings on choir techniques, organization, and philosophy have appeared frequently in the Choristers Guild *Letters*. His choral music appears in the catalogs of Chantry Music Press, Augsburg Fortress, Cambiata Press, AMSI and Choristers Guild. He has been a featured clinician at many church and school workshops dealing with all facets of music ministry both in the United States and Canada. Active in the work of the Methodist church nationally, Dr. Yarrington served as President of the Fellowship of United Methodists in Music, Worship and the Other Arts (1987-1989).

REPERTOIRE LIST

Unison/canon

Title	Composer	Publisher	Code
All Praise to Thee	Tallis/Pooler	Augsburg Fortress	11-1813
Billings in the Round	Terri,ed.	Alfred	51915
Come and Be Joyful	Hopson	Genevox	4560-61
Communion Prayer	Pote	Hinshaw	HMC 436
Covenant	Yarrington	Augsburg Fortress	11-2420
Every Morning's Sun	Page	Choristers Guild	CGA-193
Everywhere I Go	Sleeth	Choristers Guild	CGA-171
God of Great and God of Small	Sleeth	Carl Fischer	CM 7808
Hallelujah, Glory Hallelujah	Sleeth	Lorenz	S-5768
Harvest of Faith, The	Lovelace	Hope	AG 7202
I Come with Joy	Lovelace	Augsburg Fortress	11-1697
Lord, Lead Us Day by Day	Handel/Hopson	Hope	HH 3908
On Eagle's Wings	Joncas	North Am. Lit.	JO-01
Open Thou My Lips	Ramseth	Augsburg Fortress	11-9324
Praise to the Lord	Jothen	Beckenhorst	BP 1-82
Psalm 150	Lovelace	Brodt	521
Saw Ye My Savior	Johnson, D. N.	Augsburg Fortress	11-1732
Singing Glory Hallelujah	Sleeth	Lorenz	S-5768
Sunday Rounds	Parker	Hinshaw	HMC 106
Wake Up, My Soul	Hopson	Carl Fischer	CM810

Two Part

Title	Composer	Publisher	Code
Brightest and Best	Sjolund	Hinshaw	HMC 544
Christ the Glory	Lallouette/Proulx	GIA	G-2288
Come, Jesus, Holy Son of God	Handel/Hopson	Shawnee	A 5623
Da Pacem Domine (SA div.)	Franck/Goetze	Boosey	6187
For the Beauty of the Earth	Hopson	Augsburg Fortress	11-2062
Gift of Love, The	Hopson	Hope	CF 148
Hear My Words	Paulus	Hinshaw	HMC 201
I See the Morning Breaking	Pote	Hinshaw	HMC 532
If Thou But Suffer God	Lindh	Concordia	98-2081
In Thee Do I Put My Trust	Beebe	Hinshaw	HMC 188
Keep Me Faithfully in Thy Paths	Handel/Proulx	GIA	G-2355
Know That the Lord Is God	Handel/Pfautsch	Alfred	872

83

Lord Is a Mighty God, The	Mendelssohn/ Hopson	Hope	A 540
O Thou Eternal Christ	Yarrington	Chantry	COA 7762
Prayer for Guidance	Pote	Hinshaw	HMC 244
Promised Land	Sleeth	Lorenz	S-5775
Sing to the Lord	Medema	Word	CS-2709
Sing Ye Joyfully	Besig	Shawnee	EA-5033
Song of Praise and Thanksgiving, A	Pote	Hinshaw	HMC183
They Shall Soar Like Eagles	Manzo	Spectra	BG 2023
Torches	Joubert	Presser	0514-30
With Songs of Rejoicing	Bach/Hopson	Carl Fischer	CM 8086
Wondering	Marshall	Hope	RS 7702
Your Love Is Finer than Life	Haugen	GIA	G-2658

Three Part

Carry Me Over	Reilly	Augsburg Fortress	11-2442
Christ Is Made the Sure Foundation	Wood	Belwin	SCHCHO6208
Come Bless Ye the Lord	Telemann/Ehret	Shawnee	D5229
Dona Nobis Pacem	Hopson arr.	Hope	HH3903
Down By the Riverside	Shaw arr.	Hal Leonard	0865 6896
Ezekiel Saw the Wheel	Martin	Hinshaw	HMC 473
Fairest Lord Jesus	Owen arr.	Augsburg Fortress	11-2245
Glory Alleluia	Crocker	Jenson	423-07040
Go Into the World	Sleeth	Choristers Guild	CGA-209
Go Tell it On the Mountain	Emerson	Jenson	403-07220
He Was Despised	Graun	Presser	352-00400
I Will Lift Up My Eyes	Carter	Hinshaw	HMC 810
Immortal Love, Forever Full	Dietterich	Hope	AP 214
Instruments Waken	Buxtehude	Concordia	98-1422
Let Me Ride	Emerson	Jenson	403-12080
Let Joyful Anthems Rise	Handel/Hopson	Shawnee	D5261
Let the Praise Go Round	Boyce/Hopson	Belwin	GCMRO3375
Like As a Father	Cherubini/ Lovelace	Choristers Guild	A-156
Liturgical Suite	Butler	Carl Fischer	CM 7752
Lonesome Valley	Martin	Hinshaw	HMC 476
Lord, in Thy Tender Mercy	Gluck	Jenson	W3768
Love Is a Song	Sleeth	Hinshaw	HMC 186
Love of God Flows Deep and Strong	Page	Hinshaw	HMC 476
Mary on a Mountain	Carter	Hinshaw	HMC 563
O Sing My Soul, Your Maker's Praise	Pote	Lorenz	S 7441

84

Power and the Glory, The	Eilers	Jenson	402-16010
Praise the Lord	Handel/Hopson	Shawnee	D5225
Praise to the Lord, Alleluia!	Carter	Presser	392-41416
Rejoice in the Lord	Viadana/Razey	Carl Fischer	CM48083
Shepherd Alleluia	Harris	Kimmel Publ.	1107-519
Sing and Be Joyful	Wilson-Knox	Belwin	SV7832
Sing Forth, Believers	Lotti/Hopson	Jenson	433-19050
Sound Forth the Trumpet in Zion	Morley/Proulx	GIA	G 1867
Truly the Lord Is Good	Mozart/Hopson	Bourne	B377845
Water Is Wide, The	Martin	Hinshaw	HMC 642
When Christ Comes to Die	Hopson	Shawnee	D5239

Four Part

Agnus Dei	Gabrieli/McCray	Cambiata	M97682
All Things Bright and Beautiful	Englert	Shawnee	A5727
Amen, Praise and Honor	Telemann/Peek	Hope	MW1222
Ave Verum Corpus	Mozart	Chantry	CLA 609
Because You Are God's Chosen Ones	Smith	Hope	A493
Cantate Domino	Pitoni/Greyson	Bourne	ES5
Church Within Us, The	Schneider/Hustad	Hope	CF105
Clap Your Hands	Roberts	Genevox	4561-69
Clap Your Hands and Sing	Pote	Hinshaw	HMC 920
Come, O Jesus	Cherubini/Ehret	Plymouth	SC16
Come, Ye that Love the Lord	Parker	Alfred	51309
Create in Me, God, a Clean Heart	Rolle/Alwes	Augsburg Fortress	114634
Cry Out and Shout	Nystedt	Summy	705
El Shaddai	Lojeski, arr.	Hal Leonard	08306465
Every Valley	Beck	Beckenhorst	BP 1040
Fling Wide the Door	Yarrington	Augsburg Fortress	11-2394
Followers of the Lamb	Dietterich	Hope	AG 7223
Forgive Our Sins as We Forgive	Lovelace	Belwin	GCMR03419
Four Motets	Tye	Hinshaw	RSCM 508
Four Psalms	Schütz	Chantry	CLA 508
Friends	Emerson, arr.	Jenson	403-06174
Gather at the Gate	Ramseth	Augsburg Fortress	11-2100
Gloria	Althouse	Shawnee	A1806
Go and Tell John	Pfautsch	Hope	CY 3334
Go Tell It on the Mountain	Sjolund arr.	Hinshaw	HMC 543
God So Loved the World	Nygard	Presser	392414
Gracious Spirit, Holy Ghost	Williams	AMSI	281
Hodie! Emmanuel! Gloria!	Price	Hinshaw	HMC 157

Hosanna, Sing Praise!	Pethel	Lorenz	TUM 311
How Majestic Is Your Name	Lojeski, arr.	Hal Leonard	08320244
I Have Longed for Thy Saving Health	Byrd/Whitehead	Belwin	GCMR01679
I Was Glad	Hastings	Bourne	061776
I Will Arise	Parker	Alfred	905
I Will Give Thanks	Pote	Augsburg Fortress	11-9927
I'm But a Stranger Here	Martin	Hinshaw	HMC 640
In the Shadow of Your Wings	Medema	Spectra	RH 0709
Is Any Afflicted, Let Him Pray	Billings	Presser	362-03185
Jazz Gloria	Sleeth	Carl Fischer	CM 7752
Jesus, Sun of Life	Handel/Bunjes	Concordia	98-1445
Joumey Is Our Home, The	Pote	Hinshaw	HMC 446
Kum Ba Yah	Lojeski, arr.	Hal Leonard	08340000
Lead Me Lord	Wesley/Young	Hope	RS 7701
Let the People Praise	Red	Word	CS 2875
Lone Wild Bird, The	Johnson	Augsburg Fortress	11-0522
Lord, Listen to Your Children	Medema/Schrader	Hope	GC 850
Lord, What Is Man	Parker	Alfred	51321
Make a Joyful Noise	Pote	Lorenz	S 213
Many Gifts, One Spirit	Pote	Presser	392-41388
Mary, Mary	Avery & Marsh/Pfautsch	Hope	APM 892
Morning	Medema/Allen	Jenson	479-13064
Now Thank We All Our God	Pachelbel/Lovelace	Brodt	524
O Come Sing Unto the Lord	Englert	Richmond	M1-213
O Dearest Lord, Thy Sacred Head	Johnson	Augsburg Fortress	11-1607
O God of Youth	Pote	Choristers Guild	CGA-369
O Jesus I Have Promised	Carter	Hinshaw	HMC 510
O Savior of the World	Yarrington	Chantry	COA 8475
O Sons and Daughters of the King	Sjolund	Hinshaw	HMC 553
On God and Not on Human Trust	Pachelbel/Lovelace	Concordia	98-1006
Prepare the Way of the Lord	Rowan	Hope	A 596
Psallite	Praetorius	Presser	352-00139
Psalm 98	Shaw	Hal Leonard	8716191
Psalm Folksong, A	Penhorwood	Hinshaw	HMC 534
Rejoice, the Lord Is King	Hancock	Genevox	4552-81
Rise, Shine	Wood	Augsburg Fortress	11-1851
Set Down Servant	Shaw, arr.	Shawnee	A29

Show Me Thy Ways	Pelz	Augsburg Fortress	11-0642
Sing Hosanna	Shaw	Hal Leonard	08663551
Sing a New Song	Schütz/Jennings	Belwin	SCHCHO7601
Sing for Joy	Pote	Choristers Guild	CGA 161
Sing Joyous Christians	Lotti	Concordia	98-1456
Sing Praises	Pfautsch	Alfred	51367
Sing to the Lord	Tye/Davies	Ch Homeyer	HO 380
Singing Glory Hallelujah	Pote	Hinshaw	HMC 221
Song of Promise	Pote	Lorenz	S385
Street Corner Spirituals	Parker	Alfred	51594
To the House of the Lord	Yarrington	Augsburg Fortress	11-2092
Two Mozart Kyrie Settings	Mozart/McCray	Shawnee	A-17
Walk Along Beside Me, O My Lord	Besig	Shawnee	A5811
When Jesus Wept	Billings	Presser	352-00102

Cantatas, Collections, and Musicals

Barbecue for Ben	Marsh	Hope	593
Calls to Prayer, Praise, Benediction	Yarrington	Chantry	Lit-726
Command Thine Angel to Appear	Buxtehude	Chantry	CLC 532
Communion Service	Grenier	Presser	392-41448
Creation (A Rock Cantata)	Bobrowitz/Porter	Walton	WM-114
Have You Seen My Lord	Ramseth	Augsburg Fortress	11-9226
Holy Is the Lord	Hammerschmidt/ Mueller	Concordia	97-6314
obbligato C inst.			97-4481
obbligato Bb inst.			97-4482
cello			97-4483
In Dulci Jubilo	Buxtehude	Belwin	KO6131
Lord Thou Knowest All Our Being	Hammerschmidt/ Mueller	Concordia	97-5028
O Beloved Shepherds	Hammerschmidt/ Mueller	Concordia	97-6332
obbligato C inst.			97-4484
obbligato Bb inst.			97-4485
cello			97-4486
Reason to Rejoice, A	Pote	Sacred Music Press	CS79
Responses for the Church Year	Yarrington	Chantry	LIT 7811
Season to Celebrate, A	Pote	Hinshaw	HMB144
Seasonal Responses for Unison Voices	Hillert	Concordia	97-5120
Service Music for Choir and Congregation	Lovelace	Lorenz	S179
Share the Good News; (He Is Born)	Pote	Choristers Guild	CGCA 450

Share the Good News; (He Is Risen)	Pote	Choristers Guild	CGCA 500
Story-Tellin' Man, The	Medema	Word	37766
Sunday Songbook	Sleeth	Hinshaw	HMB 102
Ten Folksongs and Spirituals	Johnson	Augsburg Fortress	11-9491
Therefore Watch That Ye Be Ready	Hammerschmidt/ Mueller	Concordia	97-6316
violin part			97-4489
cello part			97-4490
Twelve Folksongs and Spirituals	Johnson	Augsburg Fortress	11-9505
Where Is the Newborn King?	Hammerschmidt/ Mueller	Concordia	97-5038
inst. parts			97-5112

BIBLIOGRAPHY

CHANGING VOICE

Cooksey, John M. "The Development of a Contemporary, Eclectic Theory for the Training and Cultivation of the Junior High School Male Changing Voice." Parts 1, 2, 3. *Choral Journal* (Oct.-Dec. 1977).

Cooper, Irvin. *Changing Voices in Junior High.* Pamphlet. New York: Carl Fischer, 1953.

Cooper, Irvin, and Keursteiner, Karl O. *Teaching Junior High School Music.* Conway, Ark.: Cambiata Press, 1967.

Mayer, Frederick D., and Sacher, Jack. "The Changing Voice." *American Choral Review* 6 (2, 3) (1965).

McKenzie, Duncan. *Training the Boy's Changing Voice.* New Brunswick, N.J.: Rutgers University Press, 1956.

Nordholm, Harriet, and Bakewell, Ruth V. *Keys to Teaching Junior High School Music.* Minneapolis: Schmitt, Hall & McCreary, 1953.

Swanson, Frederick J. *The Male Singing Voice Ages Eight to Eighteen.* Cedar Rapids, Iowa: Laurance Press, 1977.

CHORAL AND CHURCH MUSIC

Christensen, Helga. *Better Choir Singing.* Dallas, Tex.: Choristers Guild, 1973.

Davison, Archibald T. *Choral Conducting.* Cambridge, Mass.: Harvard University Press, 1962.

Decker, Harold A., and Herford, Julius. *Choral Conducting: A Symposium.* Rev. ed. Englewood Cliffs, N.J.: Prentice-Hall, 1988.

Lovelace, Austin C., and Rice, William C. *Music and Worship in the Church.* Rev. ed. Nashville, Tenn.: Abingdon, 1976.

Parker, Alice. *Creative Hymn Singing,* 2nd edition. Chapel Hill, N.C.: Hinshaw, 1976.

Robinson, Ray, and Winold, Allen. *The Choral Experience.* New York: Harper's College Press, 1976.

Routley, Erik. *Music Leadership in the Church.* Nashville, Tenn.: Abingdon, 1967.

Shewan, Robert. *Voice Training for the High School Chorus.* West Nyack, N.Y.: Parker Publishing Co., 1973.

Ulrich, Homer. *A Survey of Choral Music.* New York: Harcourt Brace Jovanovich, 1973.

DICTION

Decker, Harold A., and Kirk, Colleen J. *Choral Conducting. Focus on Communication.* Englewood Cliffs, N.J.: Prentice Hall, 1988.

Marshall, Madeleine. *The Singer's Manual of English Diction.* New York: G. Schirmer, 1953.

Pfautsch, Lloyd. *English Diction for the Singer.* New York: Lawson-Gould, 1971.

Uris, Dorothy. *To Sing in English: A Guide to Improved Diction.* New York: Boosey and Hawkes, 1971.

VOICE

Appleman, Ralph D. *The Science of Vocal Pedagogy.* Bloomington, Ind.: Indiana University Press, 1967.

DeYoung, Richard. *The Singer's Art.* Waukegan, Ill.: North Shore Press, 1958.

Fuchs, Viktor. *The Art of Singing and Voice Technique.* Reprinted. New York: London House and Maxwell, 1967.

Kagen, Sergius. *On Studying Singing.* New York: Dover Publications, 1950.

Klein, Joseph J. *Singing Technique. How to Avoid Vocal Trouble.* Princeton, N.J.: D. Van Nostrand, 1967.

McKinney, James C. *The Diagnosis and Correction of Vocal Faults.* Nashville: Broadman Press, 1982.

Nicoll, Irene Howland, and Dennis, Charles M. *Simplified Vocal Training.* New York: Carl Fischer, 1940.

Reid, Cornelius L. *Bel Canto Principles and Practices.* New York: Coleman-Ross Co., 1950.

Rosewall, Richard B. *Handbook of Singing.* Evanston, Ill.: Dickerson Press, 1984.

Rosewall, Richard B. *So Good a Thing.* Evanston, Ill.: Dickerson Press, 1984.

Stanley, Douglas. *Your Voice. Applied Science of Vocal Art.* New York: Pitman Pub., 1950.

Vennard, William. *Singing: The Mechanism and the Technic.* Rev. ed. New York: Carl Fischer, 1964.

Westerman, Kenneth N. *Emergent Voice.* Order from Carol Westerman, Box 62, Ann Arbor, Mich. Ann Arbor, Mich.: 1955.

Whitlock, Weldon. *Bel Canto for the Twentieth Century.* Champaign, Ill.: Pro Musica Press, 1968.